MEXICAN

cooking

Pictured on the front cover: Shredded Beef Fajitas *(page 104)*.
Pictured on the back cover *(top to bottom):* Chipotle Taco Filling *(page 82),* Chili Con Queso *(page 34)* and Fire and Ice *(page 184)*.

Illustrated by Anne Crosse.

ISBN-13: 978-1-4127-2415-9
ISBN-10: 1-4127-2415-5

Library of Congress Control Number: 2005920746

Manufactured in China.

8 7 6 5 4 3 2 1

Microwave Cooking: Microwave ovens vary in wattage. Use the cooking times as guidelines and check for doneness before adding more time.

Preparation/Cooking Times: Preparation times are based on the approximate amount of time required to assemble the recipe before cooking, baking, chilling or serving. These times include preparation steps such as measuring, chopping and mixing. The fact that some preparations and cooking can be done simultaneously is taken into account. Preparation of optional ingredients and serving suggestions is not included.

Contents

First Impressions

TORTILLA PIZZETTES

Makes about 30 pizzettes

  1 cup chunky salsa
  1 cup refried beans
  2 tablespoons chopped fresh cilantro
½ teaspoon ground cumin
  3 (10-inch) flour tortillas
  1 cup (4 ounces) shredded Mexican cheese blend

1. Pour salsa into strainer; let drain at least 20 minutes.

2. Meanwhile, combine refried beans, cilantro and cumin in small bowl; mix well. Preheat oven to 400°F. Spray baking sheet lightly with nonstick cooking spray; set aside.

3. Cut each tortilla into 2½-inch circles with round cookie cutter (9 to 10 circles per tortilla). Spread each tortilla circle with refried bean mixture, leaving ¼ inch around edge. Top each with a heaping teaspoonful drained salsa; sprinkle with about 1½ teaspoons cheese.

4. Place pizzettes on prepared baking sheet. Bake about 7 minutes or until tortillas are golden brown.

Tortilla Pizzettes

CLASSIC GUACAMOLE

Makes about 2 cups

4 tablespoons finely chopped white onion, divided

1 or 2 fresh serrano or jalapeño peppers,* seeded and finely chopped

1 tablespoon plus 1½ teaspoons coarsely chopped fresh cilantro, divided

¼ teaspoon chopped garlic (optional)

2 large ripe avocados

1 medium tomato, peeled and chopped

1 to 2 teaspoons fresh lime juice

¼ teaspoon salt

Packaged corn tortilla chips

Chilies and cilantro sprig for garnish (optional)

Serrano and jalapeño peppers can sting and irritate the skin; wear rubber gloves when handling peppers and do not touch eyes. Wash hands after handling.

1. Combine 2 tablespoons onion, peppers, 1 tablespoon cilantro and garlic, if desired, in large mortar. Grind with pestle until almost smooth. (Mixture can be processed in blender, if necessary, but it may become more watery than desired.)

2. Cut avocados lengthwise into halves; remove and discard pits. Scoop out avocado flesh; place in bowl. Add pepper mixture. Mash roughly, leaving avocado slightly chunky.

3. Add tomato, lime juice, salt and remaining 2 tablespoons onion and 1½ teaspoons cilantro to avocado mixture; mix well. Serve immediately or cover and refrigerate up to 4 hours. Serve with tortilla chips. Garnish, if desired.

Classic Guacamole

CALIFORNIA QUESADILLAS

Makes 8 appetizer servings

1 small ripe avocado
2 packages (3 ounces each) cream cheese, softened
3 tablespoons *Frank's® RedHot®* Original Cayenne Pepper Sauce
¼ cup minced fresh cilantro leaves
16 (6-inch) flour tortillas (2 packages)
1 cup (4 ounces) shredded Cheddar or Monterey Jack cheese
½ cup finely chopped green onions
Sour cream (optional)

Halve avocado and remove pit. Scoop out flesh into food processor or bowl of electric mixer. Add cream cheese and *Frank's RedHot* Sauce. Cover and process or beat until smooth. Add cilantro; process or beat until well blended. Spread rounded tablespoon avocado mixture onto each tortilla. Sprinkle half the tortillas with cheese and onions, dividing evenly. Top with remaining tortillas; press gently.

Place tortillas on oiled grid. Grill over medium coals 5 minutes or until cheese melts and tortillas are lightly browned, turning once. Cut into triangles. Serve with sour cream, if desired. Garnish as desired.

Note: You may serve avocado mixture as a dip with tortilla chips.

Prep Time: 20 minutes
Cook Time: 5 minutes

California Quesadillas

BELL PEPPER NACHOS

Makes 8 servings

Nonstick cooking spray
1 medium green bell pepper
1 medium yellow or red bell pepper
2 Italian plum tomatoes, seeded and chopped
⅓ cup finely chopped onion
1 teaspoon chili powder
½ teaspoon ground cumin
1½ cups cooked white rice
½ cup (2 ounces) shredded reduced-fat Monterey Jack cheese
¼ cup chopped fresh cilantro
2 teaspoons jalapeño pepper sauce *or* ¼ teaspoon hot pepper sauce
½ cup (2 ounces) shredded reduced-fat sharp Cheddar cheese

1. Spray large nonstick baking sheets with cooking spray; set aside.

2. Cut bell peppers into 2×1½-inch strips; cut strips into bite-size triangles (each bell pepper strip should yield 2 or 3 triangles).

3. Spray large nonstick skillet with cooking spray. Add tomatoes, onion, chili powder and cumin. Cook over medium heat 3 minutes or until onion is tender, stirring occasionally. Remove from heat. Stir in rice, Monterey Jack cheese, cilantro and pepper sauce.

4. Top each pepper triangle with approximately 2 tablespoons rice mixture; sprinkle with Cheddar cheese. Place on prepared baking sheets; cover with plastic wrap. Refrigerate up to 8 hours before serving.

5. When ready to serve, preheat broiler. Remove plastic wrap. Broil nachos, 6 to 8 inches from heat, 3 to 4 minutes (or bake at 400°F 8 to 10 minutes) or until cheese is bubbly and rice is heated through. Transfer to serving plate; garnish, if desired.

Bell Pepper Nachos

AVOCADOS WITH TOMATO RELISH

Makes 4 servings

1 tablespoon cider vinegar
1 tablespoon fresh orange juice
1 teaspoon grated orange peel
¼ teaspoon salt
    Dash black pepper
3 tablespoons olive oil
3 fresh plum tomatoes (about ½ pound), seeded and chopped
¼ cup coarsely chopped fresh cilantro
2 tablespoons finely chopped mild red onion
1 fresh jalapeño pepper,* seeded and finely chopped
2 large ripe avocados
2 cups shredded iceberg lettuce
    Cilantro sprig, orange peel and tomato slice for garnish (optional)

Jalapeño peppers can sting and irritate the skin; wear rubber gloves when handling peppers and do not touch eyes. Wash hands after handling.

1. Mix vinegar, orange juice, orange peel, salt and black pepper in medium bowl. Gradually add oil, whisking continuously, until dressing is thoroughly blended.

2. Add tomatoes, chopped cilantro, onion and jalapeño pepper to dressing; toss lightly to mix. Let stand, covered, at room temperature up to 2 hours to blend flavors.

3. Just before serving, cut avocados lengthwise into halves; remove and discard pits. Pare avocados and cut lengthwise into ½-inch-thick slices.

4. Arrange avocados over lettuce-lined plates; top with tomato relish. Garnish, if desired.

SOUTHWESTERN CHILI CHEESE EMPANADAS

Makes 32 appetizers

¾ cup (3 ounces) finely shredded taco-flavored cheese*
⅓ cup diced green chilies, drained
1 package (15 ounces) refrigerated pie crusts
1 egg
1 tablespoon water
Chili powder

If taco-flavored cheese is unavailable, toss ¾ cup shredded marbled Monterey Jack cheese with ½ teaspoon chili powder.

1. Combine cheese and chilies in small bowl.

2. Unfold 1 pastry crust on floured surface. Roll into 13 inch circle. Cut dough into 16 rounds using 3-inch cookie cutter, rerolling scraps as necessary. Repeat with remaining crust to total 32 circles.

3. Spoon 1 teaspoon cheese mixture in center of each dough round. Fold round in half, sealing edge with tines of fork.

4. Place empanadas on wax paper-lined baking sheets; freeze, uncovered, 1 hour or until firm. Place in resealable plastic food storage bags. Freeze up to 2 months, if desired.

5. To complete recipe, preheat oven to 400°F. Place frozen empanadas on ungreased baking sheet. Beat egg and water in small bowl; brush on empanadas. Sprinkle with chili powder.

6. Bake 12 to 17 minutes or until golden brown. Remove from baking sheet to wire rack to cool.

Serving suggestion: Serve empanadas with salsa and sour cream.

Make-Ahead Time: up to 2 months in freezer
Final Prep Time: 30 minutes

HEARTY NACHOS

Makes 8 servings

1 pound ground beef
1 envelope LIPTON® RECIPE SECRETS® Onion Soup Mix
1 can (19 ounces) black beans, rinsed and drained
1 cup prepared salsa
1 package (8½ ounces) plain tortilla chips
1 cup shredded Cheddar cheese (about 4 ounces)

1. In 12-inch nonstick skillet, brown ground beef over medium-high heat; drain.

2. Stir in soup mix, black beans and salsa. Bring to a boil over high heat. Reduce heat to low and simmer 5 minutes or until heated through.

3. Arrange tortilla chips on serving platter. Spread beef mixture over chips; sprinkle with Cheddar cheese. Top, if desired, with sliced green onions, sliced pitted ripe olives, chopped tomato and chopped cilantro.

CHILI-CHEESE QUESADILLAS WITH SALSA CRUDA

Makes 4 servings

2 tablespoons part-skim ricotta cheese
6 (6-inch) corn tortillas
½ cup (2 ounces) shredded reduced-fat Monterey Jack cheese
2 tablespoons diced mild green chilies
   Nonstick cooking spray
   Salsa Cruda (recipe follows)

Spread 2 teaspoons ricotta over 1 tortilla. Sprinkle with heaping tablespoonful Monterey Jack cheese and 2 teaspoons diced chilies. Top with another tortilla. Repeat to make 2 more quesadillas. Spray small nonstick skillet with cooking spray. Heat over medium-high heat. Add 1 quesadilla; cook 2 minutes or until bottom is golden. Turn quesadilla over; cook 2 minutes. Remove from heat. Cut into 4 wedges. Repeat with remaining quesadillas. Serve warm with Salsa Cruda.

Salsa Cruda: In small bowl, combine 1 cup chopped tomato, 2 tablespoons minced onion, 2 tablespoons minced fresh cilantro, if desired, 2 tablespoons lime juice, ½ jalapeño pepper, seeded and minced, and 1 minced garlic clove. Stir to combine. Makes 4 servings.

Hearty Nachos

FESTIVE TACO CUPS

Makes 36 taco cups

    1 tablespoon vegetable oil
    ½ cup chopped onion
    ½ pound ground turkey or ground beef
    1 clove garlic, minced
    ½ teaspoon dried oregano leaves
    ½ teaspoon chili powder or taco seasoning
    ¼ teaspoon salt
    1¼ cups shredded taco-flavored cheese or Mexican cheese blend, divided
    1 can (11½ ounces) refrigerated corn breadstick dough
       Chopped fresh tomato and sliced green onion for garnish (optional)

1. Heat oil in large skillet over medium heat. Add onion and cook until tender. Add turkey; cook until turkey is no longer pink, stirring occasionally. Stir in garlic, oregano, chili powder and salt. Remove from heat and stir in ½ cup cheese; set aside.

2. Preheat oven to 375°F. Lightly grease 36 miniature (1¾-inch) muffin pan cups. Remove dough from container but do not unroll dough. Separate dough into 8 pieces at perforations. Divide each piece into 3 pieces; roll or pat each piece into 3-inch circle. Press circles into prepared muffin pan cups.

3. Fill each cup with 1½ to 2 teaspoons turkey mixture. Bake 10 minutes. Sprinkle tops of taco cups with remaining ¾ cup cheese; bake 2 to 3 minutes more until cheese is melted. Garnish with tomato and green onion, if desired.

Festive Taco Cups

GARDEN FRESH GAZPACHO

Makes 6 servings (6 cups)

4 large tomatoes (about 2 pounds)
1 large cucumber, peeled and seeded
½ red bell pepper, seeded
½ green bell pepper, seeded
½ red onion
3 cloves garlic
¼ cup *Frank's® RedHot®* Original Cayenne Pepper Sauce
¼ cup red wine vinegar
3 tablespoons olive oil
2 tablespoons minced fresh basil
1 teaspoon salt
   Additional 2 cups chopped mixed fresh vegetables, such as tomatoes, bell peppers, cucumbers and green onions

1. Coarsely chop 4 tomatoes, 1 cucumber, ½ red bell pepper, ½ green bell pepper, ½ red onion and garlic; place in food processor or blender. Add ***Frank's RedHot*** Sauce, vinegar, oil, basil and salt. Cover; process until very smooth. (Process in batches if necessary.) Transfer soup to large glass serving bowl.

2. Stir in additional chopped vegetables, leaving some for garnish, if desired. Cover; refrigerate 1 hour before serving.

Notas

Gazpacho is a spicy Spanish soup that is served cold. It is made of a puréed mixture of fresh tomatoes, green bell peppers, onions and cucumbers. It is most often flavored with garlic, olive oil and vinegar. This refreshing summer soup is often served garnished with croutons, chopped tomato, chopped green bell pepper and green onion slices.

Garden Fresh Gazpacho

MEXICAN ROLL-UPS

Makes 12 appetizers

  6 uncooked lasagna noodles
  ¾ cup prepared guacamole
  ¾ cup chunky salsa
  ¾ cup (3 ounces) shredded fat-free Cheddar cheese
  Additional salsa (optional)

1. Cook lasagna noodles according to package directions, omitting salt. Rinse with cool water; drain. Cool.

2. Spread 2 tablespoons guacamole onto each noodle; top each with 2 tablespoons salsa and 2 tablespoons cheese.

3. Roll up noodles jelly-roll fashion. Cut each roll-up in half to form two equal-size roll-ups. Serve immediately with additional salsa, if desired, or cover with plastic wrap and refrigerate up to 3 hours.

Health Note: Ten percent of the sodium in American diets comes from natural foods, 75 percent comes from processed and canned goods, and the remaining 15 percent is added during cooking or at the table.

NACHOS À LA ORTEGA®

Makes 4 to 6 servings

  1 can (16 ounces) ORTEGA® Refried Beans, warmed
  4 cups baked tortilla chips
  1½ cups (6 ounces) shredded Monterey Jack cheese
  2 tablespoons ORTEGA Jalapeños, sliced

SUGGESTED TOPPINGS
  ORTEGA Salsa-Thick & Chunky, sour cream, guacamole, sliced ripe olives, chopped green onions, chopped fresh cilantro (optional)

PREHEAT broiler.

SPREAD beans over bottom of large ovenproof platter or 15×10-inch jelly-roll pan. Arrange chips over beans. Top with cheese and jalapeños.

BROIL for 1 to 1½ minutes or until cheese is melted. Top with desired toppings.

Mexican Roll-Ups

TORTILLA "PIZZA"

Makes 4 servings

1 can (10 ounces) chunk white chicken in water, drained
1 can (14½ ounces) Mexican-style stewed tomatoes, drained
1 green onion, minced
2 teaspoons cumin, divided
½ teaspoon garlic powder
1 cup fat-free refried beans
¼ cup chopped fresh cilantro, divided
2 large or 4 small flour tortillas
1 cup (4 ounces) shredded Monterey Jack cheese with jalapeño peppers

1. Preheat broiler. Combine chicken and tomatoes in medium bowl. Add green onion, 1 teaspoon cumin and garlic powder. Mix well; set aside.

2. Mix refried beans, remaining 1 teaspoon cumin and 2 tablespoons cilantro in small bowl. Set aside.

3. Place tortillas on baking sheet. Broil 30 seconds to 1 minute per side or until crisp but not browned. Remove from oven. *Decrease oven temperature to 400°F.* Spread each tortilla evenly with bean mixture. Spoon chicken mixture over beans; top with cheese. Bake 5 minutes.

4. Reset oven temperature to broil. Broil tortillas 2 to 3 minutes or until cheese melts. Do not let tortilla edges burn. Remove from oven; top with remaining cilantro. Serve immediately. (If using large tortillas, cut each in half.)

Serving Suggestion: Serve with a green salad tossed with avocado pieces and a lemon vinaigrette.

Prep and Cook Time: 19 minutes

TEX-MEX SPRING ROLLS

Makes about 12 spring rolls

2 tablespoons vegetable oil
4 large green onions, finely chopped
1 small red bell pepper, seeded and finely chopped
5 cups shredded Romaine or iceberg lettuce
½ cup drained and rinsed canned black beans
½ cup frozen corn
¼ cup chopped fresh cilantro
3 tablespoons *Frank's® RedHot®* Original Cayenne Pepper Sauce
1 teaspoon ground cumin
½ cup (2 ounces) shredded Monterey Jack cheese
12 to 15 spring roll wrappers (6 inches), thawed if frozen*
    Nonstick cooking spray
    Creamy Corn Salsa (recipe follows)

*Available from Asian markets or in the produce section of larger supermarkets.

1. Heat oil in large nonstick skillet over medium heat. Add green onions and bell pepper; cook and stir 2 minutes or until tender. Stir in lettuce, beans, corn, cilantro, *Frank's RedHot* Sauce and cumin. Cook 3 to 5 minutes or until liquid has evaporated, stirring occasionally. Cool 15 minutes. Stir in cheese.

2. Preheat oven to 400°F. Grease large baking sheet.

3. Place 1 wrapper on work surface like a diamond, with corner at bottom, keeping remaining wrappers covered with plastic wrap. Place about 2 tablespoons filling across center. Brush edges of wrapper with cold water. Fold bottom corner of wrapper up over filling. Fold in and overlap the opposite right and left corners to form log. Continue rolling tightly up. Repeat with remaining wrappers and filling.

4. Place rolls on prepared baking sheet. Lightly spray rolls with cooking spray. Bake 15 minutes or until golden brown and crispy, turning halfway through baking time. Prepare Creamy Corn Salsa; serve warm with spring rolls.

Creamy Corn Salsa: Combine 1 cup frozen whole kernel corn, thawed and drained, ¼ cup milk and 2 tablespoons *Frank's RedHot* Sauce in blender or food processor. Cover; process until puréed. Pour into small saucepan. Stir in 2 tablespoons chopped fresh cilantro. Cook over medium heat until heated through, stirring often. Makes 1 cup salsa.

SPICY TUNA EMPANADAS

Makes 8 servings

1 (3-ounce) pouch of STARKIST Flavor Fresh Pouch® Albacore or Chunk
  Light Tuna
1 can (4 ounces) diced green chilies, drained
1 can (2¼ ounces) sliced ripe olives, drained
½ cup shredded sharp Cheddar cheese
1 chopped hard-cooked egg
  Salt and pepper to taste
¼ teaspoon hot pepper sauce
¼ cup medium thick and chunky salsa
2 packages (15 ounces each) refrigerated pie crusts
  Additional salsa

In medium bowl, place tuna, chilies, olives, cheese, egg, salt, pepper and hot
pepper sauce; toss lightly with fork. Add ¼ cup salsa and toss again; set aside.
Following directions on package, unfold pie crusts (roll out slightly with rolling pin
if you prefer thinner crust); cut 4 circles, 4 inches each, out of each crust. Place
8 circles on foil-covered baking sheets; wet edge of each circle with water. Top
each circle with ¼ cup lightly packed tuna mixture. Top with remaining circles,
stretching pastry slightly to fit; press edges together and crimp with fork. Cut slits
in top crust to vent. Bake in 425°F oven 15 to 18 minutes or until golden brown.
Cool slightly. Serve with additional salsa.

Spicy Tuna Empanadas

TURKEY HAM QUESADILLAS

Makes 8 appetizer servings

¼ **cup picante sauce or salsa**

4 **(7-inch) regular or whole wheat flour tortillas**

½ **cup shredded reduced-fat reduced-sodium Monterey Jack cheese**

¼ **cup finely chopped turkey-ham or lean ham**

¼ **cup canned diced green chilies, drained *or* 1 to 2 tablespoons chopped jalapeño peppers***

Nonstick cooking spray

Additional picante sauce or salsa for dipping (optional)

Fat-free or reduced-fat sour cream (optional)

*Jalapeño peppers can sting and irritate the skin; wear rubber gloves when handling peppers and do not touch eyes. Wash hands after handling.

1. Spread 1 tablespoon picante sauce on each tortilla.

2. Sprinkle cheese, turkey ham and chilies equally over half of each tortilla. Fold over uncovered half to make quesadilla; spray tops and bottoms of quesadillas with cooking spray.

3. Grill on uncovered grill over medium coals 1½ minutes per side or until cheese is melted and tortillas are golden brown, turning once. Quarter each quesadilla and serve with additional picante sauce and fat-free sour cream, if desired.

Notas

Quesadillas are a versatile party food. They can be made up to a day ahead and refrigerated; reheat them on a baking sheet in a 375° oven for 15 minutes.

Turkey Ham Quesadillas

TORTILLA CRUNCH CHICKEN FINGERS

Makes about 24 chicken fingers

1 envelope LIPTON® RECIPE SECRETS® Savory Herb
    with Garlic Soup Mix
1 cup finely crushed plain tortilla chips or cornflakes (about 3 ounces)
1½ pounds boneless, skinless chicken breasts, cut into strips
1 egg
2 tablespoons water
2 tablespoons I CAN'T BELIEVE IT'S NOT BUTTER!® Spread, melted

1. Preheat oven to 400°F.

2. In medium bowl, combine savory herb with garlic soup mix and tortilla chips. In
large plastic bag or bowl, combine chicken and egg beaten with water until evenly
coated. Remove chicken and dip in tortilla mixture until evenly coated; discard bag.
On 15½×10½×1-inch jelly-roll pan sprayed with nonstick cooking spray, arrange
chicken; drizzle with I Can't Believe It's Not Butter!® Spread. Bake, uncovered,
12 minutes or until chicken is thoroughly cooked. Serve with chunky salsa, if
desired.

Tip: Serve chicken with your favorite fresh or prepared salsa.

SOPES

Makes about 35 appetizer servings

4 cups masa harina flour
½ cup vegetable shortening or lard
2½ cups warm water
1 can (7 ounces) ORTEGA® Diced Green Chiles
2 tablespoons vegetable oil
Toppings: warmed ORTEGA Refried Beans, shredded mild cheddar or shredded Monterey Jack cheese, ORTEGA Salsa (any flavor), sour cream, ORTEGA Jalapeños Slices

PLACE flour in large bowl; cut in vegetable shortening with pastry blender or two knives until mixture resembles coarse crumbs. Gradually add water, kneading until smooth. Add chiles; mix well. Form dough into 35 small balls. Pat each ball into 3 inch patty, place on waxed paper.

HEAT 1 teaspoon oil in large skillet over medium-high heat for 1 to 2 minutes. Cook patties for 3 minutes on each side or until golden brown, adding additional oil as needed.

TOP with beans, cheese, salsa, dollop of sour cream and jalapeños.

Notas

Masa harina is a specially prepared corn flour used in Mexican cooking to make corn tortillas, tamales and other corn-based doughs. It is available in most large supermarkets in 5-pound bags.

BANDITO BUFFALO WINGS

Makes 6 appetizer servings

1 package (1.25 ounces) ORTEGA® Taco Seasoning Mix
12 (about 1 pound *total*) chicken wings
     ORTEGA Salsa (any flavor)

PREHEAT oven to 375°F. Lightly grease 13×9-inch baking pan.

PLACE seasoning mix in heavy-duty plastic or paper bag. Add 3 chicken wings; shake well to coat. Place wings in prepared pan. Repeat until all wings have been coated.

BAKE for 35 to 40 minutes or until no longer pink near bone. Serve with salsa for dipping.

BITE SIZE TACOS

Makes 8 appetizer servings

1 pound ground beef
1 package (1.25 ounces) taco seasoning mix
2 cups *French's®* French Fried Onions
¼ cup chopped fresh cilantro
32 bite-size round tortilla chips
¾ cup sour cream
1 cup shredded Cheddar cheese

1. Cook beef in nonstick skillet over medium-high heat 5 minutes or until browned; drain. Stir in taco seasoning mix, *¾ cup water, 1 cup* French Fried Onions and cilantro. Simmer 5 minutes or until flavors are blended, stirring often.

2. Preheat oven to 350°F. Arrange tortilla chips on foil-lined baking sheet. Top with beef mixture, sour cream, remaining onions and cheese.

3. Bake 5 minutes or until cheese is melted and onions are golden.

Prep Time: 5 minutes
Cook Time: 15 minutes

Bandito Buffalo Wings

TUNA QUESADILLA STACK

Makes 4 servings

    4 (10-inch) flour tortillas, divided
 ¼ cup plus 2 tablespoons pinto or black bean dip
    1 can (9 ounces) tuna packed in water, drained and flaked
    2 cups (8 ounces) shredded Cheddar cheese
    1 can (14½ ounces) diced tomatoes, drained
 ½ cup thinly sliced green onions
 1½ teaspoons butter or margarine, melted

1. Preheat oven to 400°F.

2. Place 1 tortilla on 12-inch pizza pan. Spread with 2 tablespoons bean dip, leaving ½-inch border. Top with one third each of tuna, cheese, tomatoes and green onions. Repeat layers twice beginning with tortilla and ending with onions.

3. Top with remaining tortilla, pressing gently. Brush with melted butter.

4. Bake 15 minutes or until cheese melts and top is lightly browned. Cool and cut into 8 wedges.

Tip: For a special touch, serve with assorted toppings such as guacamole, sour cream and salsa.

Prep and Cook Time: 25 minutes

Tuna Quesadilla Stack

Bowlful of Mexico

CHILI CON QUESO

Makes 3 cups (about 12 servings)

2 tablespoons butter or margarine
¼ cup finely chopped onion
1 clove garlic, minced
1 can (8 ounces) tomato sauce
1 can (4 ounces) diced green chilies
2 cups (8 ounces) shredded Cheddar cheese
2 cups (8 ounces) shredded Monterey Jack cheese with jalapeño peppers
Tortilla chips and crisp raw vegetable dippers

Melt butter in 3- to 4-quart pan over medium heat. Add onion and garlic; cook until onion is tender. Stir in tomato sauce and chilies; reduce heat to low. Simmer 3 minutes. Gradually add cheeses, stirring until cheeses are melted and mixture is evenly blended. Transfer to fondue pot or chafing dish; keep warm over heat source. Serve with tortilla chips and vegetable dippers.

Chili Con Queso

Chicken Tortilla Soup

Makes 4 servings

1 clove garlic, minced
1 can (14½ ounces) chicken broth
1 jar (16 ounces) mild chunky-style salsa
2 tablespoons *Frank's® RedHot®* Original Cayenne Pepper Sauce
1 package (10 ounces) fully cooked carved chicken breasts
1 can (8¾ ounces) whole kernel corn, undrained
1 tablespoon chopped fresh cilantro (optional)
1 cup crushed tortilla chips
½ cup (2 ounces) shredded Monterey Jack cheese

1. Heat *1 teaspoon oil* in large saucepan over medium-high heat. Cook garlic 1 minute or until tender. Add broth, *¾ cup water,* salsa and **Frank's RedHot** Sauce. Stir in chicken, corn and cilantro. Heat to boiling. Reduce heat to medium-low. Cook, covered, 5 minutes.

2. Stir in tortilla chips and cheese. Serve hot.

Prep Time: 5 minutes
Cook Time: 6 minutes

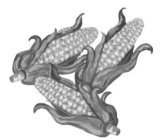

Chicken Tortilla Soup

SPICY QUICK AND EASY CHILI

Makes 4 servings

1 pound ground beef
1 large clove garlic, minced
1 can (15¼ ounces) DEL MONTE® Whole Kernel Golden Sweet Corn, drained
1 can (16 ounces) kidney beans, drained
1½ cups salsa, mild, medium or hot
1 can (4 ounces) diced green chiles, undrained

1. Brown meat with garlic in large saucepan; drain.

2. Add remaining ingredients. Simmer, uncovered, 10 minutes, stirring occasionally. Sprinkle with chopped green onions, if desired.

Prep and Cook Time: 15 minutes

Notas

Chili, often called chile con carne (Spanish for "chili with meat"), can be traced back to San Antonio where these "bowls of red" were sold in the marketplace. A thick, stewlike dish, its main ingredients are cubed or coarsely ground beef and chili peppers or chili powder. The addition of beans can be highly controversial with chili aficionados. Whereas Texans generally do not add beans, others consider beans a necessity.

Spicy Quick and Easy Chili

NACHO CHEESE SOUP

Makes 6 servings

1 package (about 5 ounces) dry au gratin potatoes
1 can (about 15 ounces) whole kernel corn, undrained
2 cups water
1 cup salsa
2 cups milk
1½ cups (6 ounces) SARGENTO® Taco Blend Shredded Cheese
1 can (about 2 ounces) sliced ripe olives, drained
    Tortilla chips (optional)

In large saucepan, combine potatoes, dry au gratin sauce mix, corn with liquid, water and salsa. Heat to a boil; reduce heat. Cover and simmer 25 minutes or until potatoes are tender, stirring occasionally. Add milk, cheese and olives. Cook until cheese is melted and soup is heated through, stirring occasionally. Garnish with tortilla chips.

VEGETABLE CHILI

Makes 4 to 6 servings

2 cans (15 ounces each) chunky chili tomato sauce
1 bag (16 ounces) BIRDS EYE® frozen Farm Fresh Mixtures Broccoli, Corn
    and Red Peppers
1 can (15½ ounces) red kidney beans
1 can (4½ ounces) chopped green chilies
½ cup shredded Cheddar cheese

• Combine tomato sauce, vegetables, beans and chilies in large saucepan; bring to a boil.

• Cook, uncovered, over medium heat 5 minutes.

• Sprinkle individual servings with cheese.

Prep Time: 5 minutes
Cook Time: 10 minutes

Nacho Cheese Soup

ALBÓNDIGAS

Makes 6 servings

1 pound lean ground beef
½ small onion, finely chopped
1 egg
¼ cup dry bread crumbs
1 tablespoon chili powder
1 teaspoon ground cumin
½ teaspoon salt
3 cans (about 14 ounces each) chicken broth
1 medium carrot, thinly sliced
1 package (10 ounces) frozen corn or thawed frozen leaf spinach
¼ cup dry sherry

1. Mix ground beef, onion, egg, bread crumbs, chili powder, cumin and salt in medium bowl until well blended. Place mixture on lightly oiled cutting board; pat evenly into 1-inch-thick square. Cut into 36 squares with sharp knife; shape each square into a ball.

2. Place meatballs slightly apart in single layer in microwavable container. Cover and cook at HIGH 3 minutes or until meatballs are no longer pink (or just barely pink) in center.

3. While meatballs are cooking, bring broth and carrot to a boil in covered Dutch oven over high heat. Stir in corn and sherry. Transfer meatballs to broth with slotted spoon. Reduce heat to medium and simmer 3 to 4 minutes or until meatballs are cooked through. (Stir in spinach, if using, and simmer until heated through.)

Note: For a special touch, sprinkle soup with chopped fresh cilantro.

Prep and Cook Time: 30 minutes

BEEF FAJITA SOUP

Makes 8 servings

1 pound beef for stew
1 can (15 ounces) pinto beans, rinsed and drained
1 can (15 ounces) black beans, rinsed and drained
1 can (14½ ounces) diced tomatoes with roasted garlic, undrained
1 can (14½ ounces) beef broth
1 small green bell pepper, thinly sliced
1 small red bell pepper, thinly sliced
1 small onion, thinly sliced
1½ cups water
2 teaspoons ground cumin
1 teaspoon seasoned salt
1 teaspoon black pepper
  Toppings: sour cream, shredded Monterey Jack or Cheddar cheese, chopped olives

SLOW COOKER DIRECTIONS

1. Combine beef, beans, tomatoes with juice, broth, bell peppers, onion, water, cumin, salt and black pepper in slow cooker.

2. Cover; cook on LOW 8 hours.

3. Serve with desired toppings.

Serving suggestion: Serve topped with sour cream, shredded Monterey Jack or Cheddar cheese and chopped olives.

TEX-MEX CHICKEN & RICE CHILI

Makes 4 servings

1 package (6.8 ounces) RICE-A-RONI® Spanish Rice
2¾ cups water
2 cups chopped cooked chicken or turkey
1 can (15 or 16 ounces) kidney beans or pinto beans, rinsed and drained
1 can (14½ or 16 ounces) tomatoes or stewed tomatoes, undrained
1 medium green bell pepper, cut into ½-inch pieces
1½ teaspoons chili powder
1 teaspoon ground cumin
½ cup (2 ounces) shredded Cheddar or Monterey Jack cheese (optional)
Sour cream (optional)
Chopped cilantro (optional)

1. In 3-quart saucepan, combine rice-vermicelli mix, Special Seasonings, water, chicken, beans, tomatoes, green pepper, chili powder and cumin. Bring to a boil over high heat.

2. Reduce heat to low; simmer, uncovered, about 20 minutes or until rice is tender, stirring occasionally.

3. Top with cheese, sour cream and cilantro, if desired.

Notas

Chili powder is a spice blend typically made up of ground dried chilies, cloves, coriander, cumin, garlic and oregano.

Tex-Mex Chicken & Rice Chili

TACO SOUP

Makes 6 servings

1 pound BOB EVANS® Original Recipe or Zesty Hot Roll Sausage
1½ tablespoons olive oil
½ small Spanish onion, diced
1 jalapeño pepper, seeded and diced
1½ cups beef broth
1 cup peeled, seeded, diced fresh or canned tomatoes
1 cup vegetable juice
½ tablespoon ground cumin
½ tablespoon chili powder
¼ teaspoon salt
⅓ cup shredded Cheddar cheese
12 tortilla chips, broken into pieces

Crumble and cook sausage in olive oil in Dutch oven until no longer pink but not yet browned. Add onion and pepper; cook until onion is tender. Add remaining ingredients except cheese and chips; bring to a boil over high heat. Reduce heat to low and simmer, uncovered, 15 minutes. Ladle soup into bowls; garnish with cheese and chips. Refrigerate leftovers.

Taco Soup

SPICY PUMPKIN SOUP WITH GREEN CHILI SWIRL

Makes 4 servings

1 can (4 ounces) diced green chilies
¼ cup reduced-fat sour cream
¼ cup fresh cilantro leaves
1 can (15 ounces) solid-pack pumpkin
1 can (14½ ounces) fat-free reduced-sodium chicken broth
½ cup water
1 teaspoon ground cumin
½ teaspoon chili powder
¼ teaspoon garlic powder
⅛ teaspoon ground red pepper (optional)
   Additional sour cream (optional)

1. Combine chilies, ¼ cup sour cream and cilantro in food processor or blender; process until smooth.*

2. Combine pumpkin, broth, water, cumin, chili powder, garlic powder and red pepper, if desired, in medium saucepan; stir in ¼ cup green chili mixture. Bring to a boil; reduce heat to medium. Simmer, uncovered, 5 minutes, stirring occasionally.

3. Pour into serving bowls. Top each serving with small dollops of remaining green chili mixture and additional sour cream, if desired. Run tip of spoon through dollops to swirl.

Omit food processor step by adding green chilies directly to soup. Finely chop cilantro and combine with sour cream. Dollop with sour cream-cilantro mixture as directed.

Notas

Fresh pumpkins can be purchased September through November. Canned pumpkin is available all year. Pumpkin seeds are dried and sold roasted and salted; they may or may not be hulled. Pumpkin seeds are used for snacking and in Mexican cooking. They are called pepitas *in Spanish.*

MEXICALI CHICKEN STEW

Makes 4 servings

1 package (1¼ ounces) taco seasoning, divided
12 ounces boneless skinless chicken thighs
  Nonstick cooking spray
2 cans (14½ ounces each) stewed tomatoes with onions, celery and green
  peppers
1 package (10 ounces) frozen corn
1 package (9 ounces) frozen green beans
4 cups tortilla chips

1. Place half of taco seasoning in small bowl. Cut chicken thighs into 1-inch pieces; coat with taco seasoning.

2. Coat large nonstick skillet with cooking spray. Cook and stir chicken 5 minutes over medium heat. Add tomatoes, corn, beans and remaining taco seasoning; bring to a boil. Reduce heat to medium-low; simmer 10 minutes. Top with tortilla chips before serving.

Serving Suggestion: Serve nachos with the stew. Spread tortilla chips on a plate; dot with salsa and sprinkle with cheese. Heat just until the cheese is melted.

Cook's Notes: To lighten up this dish, simply substitute boneless skinless chicken breasts for the thighs. Each cup of cooked light meat has 44 less calories and 8 less grams of fat than a cup of dark meat.

Prep and Cook Time: 20 minutes

POZOLE

Makes 6 servings

1 large onion, thinly sliced
1 tablespoon olive oil
2 teaspoons dried oregano leaves
1 clove garlic, minced
½ teaspoon ground cumin
2 cans (14½ ounces each) chicken broth
1 package (10 ounces) frozen corn
1 to 2 cans (4 ounces each) chopped green chilies
1 can (2¼ ounces) sliced ripe olives, drained
¾ pound boneless skinless chicken breasts
   Chopped fresh cilantro for garnish

1. Combine onion, oil, oregano, garlic and cumin in Dutch oven. Cover and cook over medium heat about 6 minutes or until onion is tender, stirring occasionally.

2. Stir broth, corn, chilies and olives into onion mixture. Cover and bring to a boil over high heat.

3. While soup is cooking, cut chicken into thin strips. Add to soup. Reduce heat to medium-low; cover and cook 3 to 4 minutes or until chicken is no longer pink. Garnish with cilantro, if desired.

Cook's Notes: A Dutch oven is a large pot or kettle with a tight-fitting lid that prevents steam from escaping while cooking.

Prep and Cook Time: 20 minutes

Pozole

SOUTH-OF-THE-BORDER CORN AND ONION SOUP

Makes 6 to 8 servings

2 cans (13¾ ounces each) chicken broth
1 package (16 ounces) frozen whole kernel corn
1 cup mild taco sauce
1⅓ cups *French's*® French Fried Onions, divided
1 tablespoon *Frank's*® *RedHot*® Original Cayenne Pepper Sauce
½ teaspoon ground cumin
1 cup (4 ounces) shredded Cheddar or Monterey Jack cheese
    with jalapeño pepper
1 can (4 ounces) chopped green chilies, drained
1 cup low-fat sour cream

Combine chicken broth, corn, taco sauce, ⅔ *cup* French Fried Onions, **Frank's RedHot** Sauce and cumin in large saucepan. Bring to a boil over high heat, stirring often. Reduce heat to low. Simmer, uncovered, 10 minutes, stirring occasionally.

Pour one third of the soup into blender or food processor. Cover tightly; blend until puréed. Transfer to large bowl. Repeat with remaining soup, blending in batches. Return all puréed mixture to saucepan.

Add cheese; whisk until cheese melts and mixture is well blended. Stir in green chilies and sour cream. Cook over low heat until heated through. Do not boil. Ladle soup into individual bowls. Garnish with additional sour cream, if desired. Sprinkle with remaining ⅔ *cup* onions.

Prep Time: 30 minutes
Cook Time: 15 minutes

South-of-the-Border Corn and Onion Soup

CHILI MOLE

Makes 6 servings

1 pound ground beef
1 Spanish onion, diced
1 green bell pepper, diced
1 banana pepper, finely chopped
2 jalapeño peppers, finely chopped*
2 cloves garlic, finely chopped
2 cans (14 ounces each) kidney beans, drained
2 cans (14 ounces each) diced tomatoes, undrained
1 can (4 ounces) tomato paste
1 packet (2 ounces) Cincinnati-style chili seasoning
3 tablespoons unsweetened cocoa powder
2 tablespoons chili powder
1 tablespoon brown sugar
1 tablespoon lime juice

Jalapeño peppers can sting and irritate the skin; wear rubber gloves when handling peppers and do not touch eyes. Wash hands after handling.

1. Brown ground beef in large Dutch oven over medium heat. Cook until no longer pink; drain off fat.

2. Add onion and bell pepper to pot; cook and stir until onion is translucent.

3. Add banana pepper, jalapeño peppers and garlic; cook and stir 3 minutes.

4. Add beans and tomatoes with juice.

5. Stir in tomato paste, chili seasoning, cocoa, chili powder, brown sugar and lime juice. Cover and simmer 1 hour.

Chili Mole

TORTILLA SOUP

Makes 6 servings

    1 tablespoon butter or margarine
 ½ cup chopped green bell pepper
 ½ cup chopped onion
 ½ teaspoon ground cumin
3½ cups (two 14½ ounce cans) chicken broth
    1 jar (16 ounces) ORTEGA® Salsa-Thick & Chunky
    1 cup whole-kernel corn
    1 tablespoon vegetable oil
    6 corn tortillas, cut into ½-inch strips
 ¾ cup (3 ounces) shredded 4 cheese Mexican blend
      Sour cream (optional)

MELT butter in medium saucepan over medium heat. Add bell pepper, onion and cumin; cook for 3 to 4 minutes or until tender. Stir in broth, salsa and corn. Bring to a boil. Reduce heat to low; cook for 5 minutes.

HEAT vegetable oil in medium skillet over medium-high heat. Add tortilla strips; cook for 3 to 4 minutes or until tender.

SERVE in soup bowls. Top with tortilla strips, cheese and a dollop of sour cream.

Notas

*A tortilla is a round, thin unleavened baked
Mexican bread. It can be made of either corn or
wheat flour, water and a little salt. Traditionally
the dough is shaped, flattened by hand and
cooked on both sides on a hot griddle until dry
and flecked with brown. Tortillas are a staple of
Mexican and Tex-Mex cooking.*

SOPA DE LIMA

Makes 6 servings

2 tablespoons extra-virgin olive oil
2 pounds chicken thighs and legs
1 cup chopped yellow onions
2 cloves garlic, minced
6 cups water
1 cup seeded and chopped tomatoes
1 jalapeño pepper, minced* *or* ¼ teaspoon dried red pepper flakes
1 tablespoon chili powder
1 teaspoon ground cumin
1 teaspoon dried oregano
3 tablespoons lime juice
2 teaspoons salt or to taste
½ cup chopped cilantro leaves
¼ cup finely chopped radishes
   Lime wedges

*Jalapeño peppers can sting and irritate the skin; wear rubber gloves when handling peppers and do not touch eyes. Wash hands after handling.

1. Place Dutch oven over medium-high heat until hot. Add oil and chicken; cook on both sides until browned, about 4 minutes total. Remove to plate.

2. Add onion and garlic to Dutch oven. Reduce heat to medium and cook 3 to 4 minutes or until onions are translucent. Increase heat to high; add water and bring to a boil. Add reserved chicken, tomatoes, jalapeño peppers, chili powder, cumin and oregano. Bring just to a boil; reduce heat, cover tightly and simmer 1 hour or until chicken is falling of the bone. Remove chicken with slotted spoon and cool slightly; remove meat from the bone, shred and return to Dutch oven with lime juice and salt.

3. Combine cilantro and radishes. Serve soup in bowl; garnish with radish mixture and lime wedges.

TACO BEAN CHILI

Makes 6 to 8 servings

½ cup dried kidney beans
½ cup dried pinto beans
½ cup dried red beans
4 cups water
1 pound ground beef or ground turkey, browned and drained
1 can (14½ ounces) diced tomatoes with green chilies, undrained
1 can (8 ounces) tomato sauce
1 package (1¼ ounces) taco seasoning mix
1 tablespoon dried minced onion
½ teaspoon chili powder *or* chipotle chili pepper seasoning
¼ teaspoon ground cumin
1½ cups tortilla chips

1. Place beans in large bowl; cover with water. Soak 6 to 8 hours or overnight. (To quick soak beans, place beans in large saucepan; cover with water. Bring to a boil over high heat. Boil 2 minutes. Remove from heat; let soak, covered, 1 hour.) Drain beans; discard water.

2. Place soaked beans, 4 cups water, ground beef, tomatoes with juice, tomato sauce, seasoning mix, onion, chili powder and cumin in Dutch oven. Bring to a boil over high heat. Cover; reduce heat and simmer 1½ to 2 hours or until beans are tender.

3. Crush tortilla chips. Stir into chili and cook 5 to 10 minutes to thicken. Serve with accompaniments, if desired.

Taco Bean Chili

PICANTE BLACK BEAN SOUP

Makes 6 to 8 servings

    4 slices bacon
    1 large onion, chopped
    1 clove garlic, minced
    2 cans (15 ounces each) black beans, undrained
    1 can (about 14 ounces) beef broth
1¼ cups water
    ¾ cup picante sauce
    ½ to 1 teaspoon salt
    ½ teaspoon dried oregano leaves
    Sour cream
    Crackers and additional picante sauce

1. Using scissors, cut through several slices of bacon at once, cutting into ½×½-inch pieces.

2. Cook and stir bacon in large saucepan over medium-high heat until crisp. Remove with slotted spoon; drain on paper towels. Set bacon aside.

3. Add onion and garlic to drippings in saucepan; cook and stir 3 minutes.

4. Add beans with liquid, broth, water, ¾ cup picante sauce, salt to taste and oregano. Reduce heat to low. Simmer, covered, 20 minutes.

5. Ladle into soup bowls; dollop with sour cream. Sprinkle with bacon. Serve with crackers and additional picante sauce.

Picante Black Bean Soup

HEARTY TORTILLA CHIP SOUP

Makes 8 servings

1 cup chopped onion
¾ cup finely chopped carrots
1 clove garlic, minced
6 ounces GUILTLESS GOURMET® Unsalted Baked Tortilla Chips
3 cans (14½ ounces each) low sodium chicken broth, defatted
2 cups water
1 cup GUILTLESS GOURMET® Roasted Red Pepper Salsa
1 can (6 ounces) low sodium tomato paste
1 cup (4 ounces) shredded low fat Monterey Jack cheese

MICROWAVE DIRECTIONS

Combine onion, carrots and garlic in 3-quart microwave-safe casserole. Cover with vented plastic wrap or lid; microwave on HIGH (100% power) 7 minutes or until vegetables are tender. Finely crush half the tortilla chips. Add crushed chips, broth, water, salsa and tomato paste; stir well. Cover; microwave on HIGH 6 minutes or until soup bubbles. Microwave on MEDIUM (50% power) 5 minutes. To serve, divide remaining tortilla chips and half the cheese among 8 individual soup bowls. Ladle soup over cheese and chips, dividing evenly. Sprinkle with remaining cheese.

Stove Top Directions: Bring 2 tablespoons broth to a boil in 3-quart saucepan over medium-high heat. Add onion, carrots and garlic; cook and stir about 5 minutes until vegetables are tender. Finely crush half the tortilla chips. Add crushed chips, remaining broth, water, salsa and tomato paste; stir well. Cook over medium heat until soup comes to a boil. Reduce heat to low; simmer 5 minutes. Serve as directed.

Hearty Tortilla Chip Soup

GRILLED STEAK CHILI

Makes 8 to 10 servings

¼ cup minced garlic

¼ cup corn oil

3 cups chopped onion

1 can (15 ounces) beef stock

3 cans (14½ ounces each) Mexican-style diced tomatoes with chilies, undrained

2 cans (15 ounces each) crushed tomatoes

¼ cup plus 2 tablespoons chili powder

2 teaspoons ground cumin

2 teaspoons dried oregano

1 teaspoon ground black pepper

4 pounds beef steak (preferably ribeye)

¼ cup masa harina (corn flour) or yellow corn meal (optional)

Minced cilantro, sliced green onions and sliced ripe olives for garnish

1. Place garlic and oil in large stock pot over low heat. Add onion; cook and stir 5 minutes. Stir in beef stock, tomatoes, chili powder, cumin, oregano and pepper; bring to a boil. Stir and reduce heat; cover and simmer 1 to 2 hours or until thick.

2. Preheat electric grill or broiler. Grill steak just until browned on both sides, about 8 minutes. Let rest 15 minutes before slicing steak into 2×½-inch strips on rimmed cutting board. Stir sliced steak and reserved juices into chili; heat 5 to 10 minutes. If a thicker chili is desired, slowly sprinkle in masa harina or corn meal; cook and stir 12 to 15 minutes or until thickened. Garnish with cilantro, onions and olives.

Grilled Steak Chili

CHUNKY VEGETABLE CHILI

Makes 8 servings

2 tablespoons vegetable oil
1 medium onion, chopped
2 ribs celery, diced
1 carrot, diced
3 cloves garlic, minced
2 cans (about 15 ounces each) Great Northern beans, rinsed and drained
1½ cups water
1 cup frozen whole kernel corn
1 can (6 ounces) tomato paste
1 can (4 ounces) diced mild green chilies, undrained
1 tablespoon chili powder
2 teaspoons dried oregano leaves
1 teaspoon salt
Cilantro for garnish

1. Heat oil in large skillet over medium-high heat until hot. Add onion, celery, carrot and garlic; cook 5 minutes or until vegetables are tender, stirring occasionally.

2. Stir beans, water, corn, tomato paste, chilies, chili powder, oregano and salt into skillet. Reduce heat to medium-low. Simmer 20 minutes, stirring occasionally. Garnish with cilantro, if desired.

Southwestern Beef Stew

Makes about 6 servings

1 tablespoon plus 1 teaspoon BERTOLLI® Olive Oil, divided
1½ pounds boneless beef chuck, cut into 1-inch cubes
1 can (4 ounces) chopped green chilies, drained
2 large cloves garlic, finely chopped
1 teaspoon ground cumin (optional)
1 can (14 to 16 ounces) whole or plum tomatoes, undrained and chopped
1 envelope LIPTON® RECIPE SECRETS® Onion or Beefy Onion Soup Mix
1 cup water
1 package (10 ounces) frozen cut okra or green beans, thawed
1 large red or green bell pepper, cut into 1-inch pieces
4 frozen half-ears corn-on-the-cob, thawed and each cut into 3 round pieces
2 tablespoons chopped fresh cilantro (optional)

In 5-quart Dutch oven or heavy saucepot, heat 1 tablespoon oil over medium-high heat and brown ½ of the beef; remove and set aside. Repeat with remaining beef; remove and set aside. In same Dutch oven, heat remaining 1 teaspoon oil over medium heat and cook chilies, garlic and cumin, stirring constantly, 3 minutes. Return beef to Dutch oven. Stir in tomatoes and onion soup mix blended with water. Bring to a boil over high heat. Reduce heat to low and simmer covered, stirring occasionally, 1 hour. Stir in okra, red pepper and corn. Bring to a boil over high heat. Reduce heat to low and simmer covered, stirring occasionally, 30 minutes or until meat is tender. Sprinkle with cilantro.

MEXICAN HOT POT

Makes 6 servings

1 tablespoon canola oil
1 onion, sliced
3 cloves garlic, minced
2 teaspoons red pepper flakes
2 teaspoons dried oregano leaves, crushed
1 teaspoon ground cumin
1 can (28 ounces) tomatoes, chopped, undrained
2 cups whole kernel corn, fresh or frozen
1 can (15 ounces) chick-peas (garbanzo beans), rinsed and drained
1 can (15 ounces) pinto beans, rinsed and drained
1 cup water
6 cups shredded iceberg lettuce

1. Heat oil in stockpot or Dutch oven over medium-high heat. Add onion and garlic; cook and stir 5 minutes. Add red pepper flakes, oregano and cumin; mix well.

2. Stir in tomatoes with juice, corn, chick-peas, pinto beans and water; bring to a boil over high heat.

3. Reduce heat to medium-low; cover and simmer 15 minutes. Top individual servings with 1 cup shredded lettuce. Serve hot.

Notas

Chili powders, ground red (cayenne) pepper and red pepper flakes are all made from dried chilies. Whether you're working with fresh, dried or ground chilies, it is important to know that the longer you cook chilies, the hotter the dish will be. That's why a long simmered stew with chilies may be quite hot, while a quick stir-fry with chilies has more flavor and less heat.

Mexican Hot Pot

SOUTHWESTERN TWO BEAN CHILI & RICE

Makes 4 servings

1 bag (about ½ cup uncooked) boil-in-bag white rice
1 tablespoon vegetable oil
1 cup chopped onion
1 cup chopped green bell pepper
1½ teaspoons bottled minced garlic
1 can (15½ ounces) chili beans in spicy or mild sauce, undrained
1 can (15½ ounces) black or pinto beans, rinsed and drained
1 can (10 ounces) diced tomatoes with green chilies, undrained
1 tablespoon chili powder
2 teaspoons ground cumin
1 cup (4 ounces) shredded Cheddar or Monterey Jack cheese

1. Cook rice according to package directions.

2. While rice is cooking, heat oil in large saucepan over medium-high heat until hot. Add onion, bell pepper and garlic. Cook 5 minutes, stirring occasionally. Stir in chili beans with sauce, black beans, tomatoes with juice, chili powder and cumin. Cover; bring to a boil over high heat. Reduce heat to medium-low. Simmer, covered, 10 minutes.

3. Transfer rice to 4 shallow bowls. Ladle bean mixture over rice; top with cheese.

Prep and Cook Time: 20 minutes

Southwestern Two Bean Chili & Rice

CRUNCHY LAYERED BEEF & BEAN SALAD

Makes 6 servings

1 pound ground beef or turkey
2 cans (15 to 19 ounces each) black beans or pinto beans,
    rinsed and drained
1 can (14½ ounces) stewed tomatoes, undrained
1⅓ cups *French's®* French Fried Onions, divided
1 tablespoon *Frank's® RedHot®* Original Cayenne Pepper Sauce
1 package (1¼ ounces) taco seasoning mix
6 cups shredded lettuce
1 cup (4 ounces) shredded Cheddar or Monterey Jack cheese

1. Cook beef in large nonstick skillet over medium heat until thoroughly browned; drain well. Stir in beans, tomatoes, ⅔ cup French Fried Onions, **Frank's RedHot** Sauce and taco seasoning. Heat to boiling. Cook over medium heat 5 minutes, stirring occasionally.

2. Spoon beef mixture over lettuce on serving platter. Top with cheese.

3. Microwave remaining ⅔ *cup* onions 1 minute on HIGH. Sprinkle over salad.

Prep Time: 10 minutes
Cook Time: 6 minutes

Crunchy Layered Beef & Bean Salad

PEPPER-SPICED BEEF SKEWERS AND BEANS

Makes 6 servings

1½ pounds beef tenderloin or boneless beef top sirloin steaks
1 large red bell pepper
1 large green bell pepper
1 large onion, halved
   Pepper-Spice Seasoning (recipe follows)
2 tablespoons lemon juice
2 teaspoons olive oil
3 cups cooked and drained Great Northern, navy or pinto beans *or* 2 cans
   (16 ounces each) beans, rinsed and drained
1 can (28 ounces) no-salt-added stewed tomatoes, drained
2 tablespoons packed brown sugar
2 tablespoons chopped fresh parsley

1. Cut beef into ¾- to 1-inch cubes. Cut bell peppers and half of onion into ¾- to 1-inch squares (you will need 24 to 30 squares of each). Thread peppers and vegetables alternately onto 6 (10- to 12-inch) metal skewers beginning with 1 piece of each vegetable followed by 1 cube meat. Prepare Pepper-Spice Seasoning; combine 2 tablespoons seasoning with lemon juice in small bowl. Brush mixture over beef cubes.

2. Spray cold grid with nonstick cooking spray. Prepare grill for direct cooking. Place skewers on grid, 4 to 6 inches from medium-hot coals. Grill 8 to 10 minutes, turning every 2 to 3 minutes, or until meat is grilled to desired doneness.

3. Meanwhile, finely chop remaining onion half. Heat oil in medium saucepan over medium-high heat. Add onion and remaining 2 tablespoons spice mixture. Cook and stir 3 minutes or until onion is tender. *(Do not let spices burn.)* Stir in beans, tomatoes and brown sugar. Cover; cook and stir until heated through. Stir in parsley.

Pepper-Spice Seasoning: Combine 2 tablespoons lemon juice, 2 tablespoons minced garlic, 2 teaspoons dried oregano, 2 teaspoons ground black pepper, 1 teaspoon ground cumin and 1 teaspoon ground allspice in small bowl; mix well. Makes ¼ cup.

Pepper-Spiced Beef Skewer and Beans

Zesty Steak Fajitas

Makes 4 servings

¾ cup *French's®* Worcestershire Sauce, divided
1 pound boneless top round, sirloin or flank steak
3 tablespoons taco seasoning mix
2 red or green bell peppers, cut into quarters
1 to 2 large onions, cut into thick slices
¾ cup chili sauce
8 (8-inch) flour or corn tortillas, heated
    Sour cream and shredded cheese (optional)

1. Pour ½ cup Worcestershire over steak in deep dish. Cover and refrigerate 30 minutes or up to 3 hours. Drain meat and rub both sides with seasoning mix.

2. Grill meat and vegetables over medium-hot coals 10 to 15 minutes until meat is medium rare and vegetables are charred, but tender.

3. Thinly slice meat and vegetables. Place in large bowl. Add chili sauce and ¼ cup Worcestershire. Toss to coat. Serve in tortillas and garnish with sour cream and cheese.

Prep Time: 5 minutes
Cook Time: 15 minutes
Marinate Time: 30 minutes

Zesty Steak Fajita

Fiesta Beef Enchiladas

Makes 6 servings

8 ounces 95% lean ground beef
½ cup sliced green onions
2 teaspoons minced garlic
1 cup cold cooked white or brown rice
1½ cups chopped tomato, divided
¾ cup frozen corn, thawed
1 cup (4 ounces) shredded reduced-fat Mexican cheese blend or Cheddar cheese, divided
½ cup salsa or picante sauce
12 (6- to 7-inch) corn tortillas
1 can (10 ounces) mild or hot enchilada sauce
1 cup shredded romaine lettuce

1. Preheat oven to 375°F. Spray 13×9-inch baking dish with nonstick cooking spray; set aside.

2. Cook ground beef in medium nonstick skillet over medium heat until no longer pink; drain. Add green onions and garlic; cook and stir 2 minutes.

3. Add rice, 1 cup tomato, corn, ½ cup cheese and salsa to meat mixture; mix well. Spoon mixture down center of tortillas. Roll up; place seam side down in prepared dish. Spoon enchilada sauce evenly over enchiladas.

4. Cover with foil; bake 20 minutes or until hot. Sprinkle with remaining ½ cup cheese; bake 5 minutes or until cheese melts. Top with lettuce and remaining ½ cup tomato.

Prep Time: 15 minutes
Cook Time: 35 minutes

Fiesta Beef Enchiladas

TAMALE PIE

Makes 6 servings

1 pound ground beef round
1 package (10 ounces) frozen corn, thawed
1 can (14½ ounces) diced tomatoes, undrained
1 can (4 ounces) sliced black olives, drained
1 package (1¼ ounces) taco seasoning mix
1 package (6 ounces) corn muffin or corn bread mix plus
   ingredients to prepare mix
¼ cup (1 ounce) shredded Cheddar cheese
1 green onion, thinly sliced

1. Preheat oven to 400°F. Place meat in large skillet; cook over high heat 6 to 8 minutes or until meat is no longer pink, breaking meat apart with wooden spoon. Pour off drippings. Add corn, tomatoes with juice, olives and seasoning mix to meat. Bring to a boil over medium-high heat, stirring constantly. Pour into deep 9-inch pie plate; smooth top with spatula.

2. Prepare corn muffin mix according to package directions. Spread evenly over meat mixture. Bake 8 to 10 minutes or until golden brown. Sprinkle with cheese and onion slices. Let stand 10 minutes before serving.

Serving Suggestion: Serve with papaya wedges sprinkled with lime juice.

Prep and Cook Time: 20 minutes

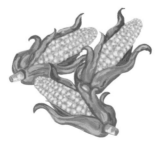

WHITE CHILI PILAF

Makes 6 servings

    Nonstick cooking spray
½ pound lean ground beef
½ pound bulk turkey sausage
 1 cup finely chopped green bell pepper
 2 to 3 tablespoons seeded, minced jalapeño peppers*
 2 teaspoons minced garlic
 2 teaspoons ground cumin
½ teaspoon dried oregano leaves
2¼ cups water
 2 teaspoons chicken flavor bouillon granules
 1 cup uncooked white basmati rice
 1 cup rinsed, drained canned Great Northern beans
 1 cup sliced green onions
½ cup minced fresh cilantro
 6 tablespoons fat-free sour cream
¾ cup diced seeded tomato
½ cup plus 1 tablespoon shredded reduced-fat Colby-Jack cheese

Jalapeño peppers can sting and irritate the skin; wear rubber gloves when handling peppers and do not touch eyes. Wash hands after handling.

1. Spray large skillet with cooking spray; heat over medium heat until hot. Add beef and sausage; cook 5 minutes or until meat is no longer pink, stirring to crumble. Remove meat from skillet.

2. Spray large saucepan with cooking spray; add peppers and garlic. Cook and stir over medium heat 5 minutes or until peppers are tender. Stir in cumin and oregano; cook and stir 1 minute. Stir in combined water and bouillon granules; bring to a boil over high heat. Stir in rice. Cover; reduce heat to medium-low. Simmer 15 minutes.

3. Add meat, beans and onions to saucepan; cover. Simmer 5 minutes or until rice is tender. Remove saucepan from heat; stir in cilantro. Cover; let stand 5 minutes. Top each serving evenly with dollop of sour cream; garnish with tomato and cheese.

CHIPOTLE TACO FILLING

Makes 8 cups filling

2 pounds ground beef chuck

2 cans (15 ounces each) pinto beans, rinsed and drained

2 cups chopped yellow onions

1 can (14½ ounces) diced tomatoes with peppers and onions, drained

4 chipotle peppers in adobo sauce, mashed

1 tablespoon sugar

1 tablespoon beef bouillon granules

1½ teaspoons ground cumin

    Taco shells or flour tortillas

SLOW COOKER DIRECTIONS

1. Brown ground beef in large nonstick skillet over medium-high heat, stirring to separate meat. Drain and discard fat.

2. Combine beef, beans, onions, tomatoes, peppers, sugar, bouillon and cumin in slow cooker. Cover; cook on LOW 4 hours or on HIGH 2 hours.

3. Serve in taco shells. Add shredded lettuce, salsa, shredded cheese and sour cream, if desired.

Notas

Chipotles are smoked, dried red jalapeño peppers. They have a rich, smoky, very hot flavor. They are commonly canned in adobo sauce.

Chipotle Taco Filling

BEEF & SALSA SALAD SUPREME

Makes 4 servings

1 boneless beef top sirloin steak (about 1 pound)
2 teaspoons Mexican seasoning blend or chili powder
1 package (8 ounces) assorted torn salad greens or mesclun salad mix
1 cup rinsed, drained canned black beans
1 cup frozen corn, thawed
¼ cup picante sauce or salsa
¼ cup red wine vinegar and oil salad dressing
1 medium tomato, chopped

1. Heat large nonstick skillet over medium heat. Rub both sides of steak with seasoning. Cook steak in skillet 5 minutes per side to medium-rare or until desired doneness. Transfer steak to carving board; tent with foil. Let stand 5 minutes.

2. While steak is cooking, combine salad greens, beans and corn in large bowl. Combine picante sauce and dressing; add to greens mixture. Toss lightly to coat. Arrange on salad plates.

3. Carve steak crosswise into ¼-inch strips; arrange over salad greens, dividing evenly. Sprinkle with chopped tomato.

Serving Suggestion: For a special touch, add a sprig of cilantro to each serving.

Prep and Cook Time: 20 minutes

Beef & Salsa Salad Supreme

STUFFED MEXICAN PIZZA PIE

Makes 6 servings

1 pound ground beef
1 large onion, chopped
1 large green bell pepper, chopped
1½ cups UNCLE BEN'S® Instant Rice
2 cans (14½ ounces each) Mexican-style stewed tomatoes, undrained
⅔ cup water
2 cups (8 ounces) shredded Mexican-style seasoned Monterey Jack-Colby
    cheese blend, divided
1 container (10 ounces) refrigerated pizza crust dough

1. Preheat oven to 425°F. Spray 13×9-inch baking pan with cooking spray;
set aside.

2. Spray large nonstick skillet with nonstick cooking spray; heat over high heat
until hot. Add beef, onion and bell pepper; cook and stir 5 minutes or until meat is
no longer pink.

3. Add rice, stewed tomatoes and water. Bring to a boil. Pour beef mixture into
prepared baking pan. Sprinkle with 1¼ cups cheese and stir until blended.

4. Unroll pizza crust dough on work surface. Place dough in one even layer over
mixture in baking pan. Cut 6 to 8 slits in dough with sharp knife. Bake 10 minutes
or until crust is lightly browned. Sprinkle top of crust with remaining ¾ cup
cheese; continue baking 4 minutes or until cheese is melted and crust is deep
golden brown.

5. Let stand 5 minutes before cutting.

Stuffed Mexican Pizza Pie

EASY FAMILY BURRITOS

Makes 8 servings

1 boneless beef chuck roast (2 to 3 pounds)
1 jar (24 ounces) *or* 2 jars (16 ounces each) salsa
 Flour tortillas

SLOW COOKER DIRECTIONS

1. Place roast in slow cooker; top with salsa. Cover; cook on LOW 8 to 10 hours.

2. Remove meat from slow cooker. Shred with 2 forks. Return to slow cooker; cook additional 1 to 2 hours.

3. Serve shredded meat wrapped in warm tortillas.

Notas

Burritos, originating in Mexico, are flour tortillas filled and folded into rectangular-shaped packages. Fillings vary and may include combinations of refried beans, shredded meat, poultry, chorizo, cheese, lettuce, tomatoes and sour cream. Breakfast burritos may be filled with seasoned scrambled eggs or a fruit mixture. Burritos are served without a sauce but may be garnished with sour cream or salsa.

Easy Family Burritos

CHILI-STUFFED POBLANO PEPPERS

Makes 4 servings

1 pound 90% lean ground beef
4 large poblano peppers
1 can (15 ounces) chili-seasoned beans
1 can (14½ ounces) chili-style chunky tomatoes, undrained
1 tablespoon Mexican (adobo) seasoning
⅔ cup shredded Mexican cheese blend or Monterey Jack cheese

1. Preheat broiler. Bring 2 quarts water to a boil in 3-quart saucepan. Cook ground beef in large nonstick skillet over medium-high heat 5 to 6 minutes or until no longer pink.

2. While meat is cooking, cut peppers in half lengthwise; remove stems and seeds. Add 4 pepper halves to boiling water; cook 3 minutes or until bright green and slightly softened. Remove; drain upside down on plate. Repeat with remaining 4 halves. Set aside.

3. Add beans, tomatoes with juice and Mexican seasoning to ground beef. Cook and stir over medium heat 5 minutes or until mixture thickens slightly.

4. Arrange peppers, cut side up, in 13×9-inch baking dish. Divide chili mixture evenly among each pepper; top with cheese. Broil 6 inches from heat 1 minute or until cheese is melted. Serve immediately.

Serving Suggestion: Serve with corn bread and chunky salsa.

Prep and Cook Time: 26 minutes

STEAK & PEPPER FAJITAS

Makes 4 servings

1 packet (1.12 ounces) fajita marinade
1 pound boneless steak,* cut into thin strips
1 bag (16 ounces) BIRDS EYE® frozen Farm Fresh Mixtures Pepper Stir
    Fry vegetables
8 (6- to 7-inch) flour tortillas, warmed
½ cup salsa

Or, substitute 1 pound boneless, skinless chicken, cut into strips.

• Prepare fajita marinade according to package directions.

• Add steak and vegetables. Let stand 10 minutes.

• Heat large skillet over medium-high heat. Remove steak and vegetables with slotted spoon and place in skillet.

• Add marinade, if desired. Cook 5 minutes or until steak is desired doneness and mixture is heated through, stirring occasionally.

• Wrap mixture in tortillas. Top with salsa.

Serving Suggestion: Serve with guacamole and sour cream, or serve mixture over rice instead of in flour tortillas.

Birds Eye Idea: Vegetables do not have to be fresh to be nutritious. Add cooked Birds Eye® broccoli or spinach to frozen pizza.

Prep Time: 10 minutes
Cook Time: 5 to 7 minutes

CARNE ASADA

Makes 4 servings

1 beef flank or round tip steak (1½ to 1¾ pounds)
½ cup lime juice
6 cloves garlic, chopped
1 teaspoon black pepper
  Salt
1 large green bell pepper, cut lengthwise into 1-inch strips
8 corn tortillas, warmed
  Tomato salsa

1. Combine steak, lime juice, garlic and black pepper in resealable plastic food storage bag; seal. Refrigerate overnight, turning at least once to marinate meat evenly.

2. Preheat broiler. Remove steak from bag and place on broiler pan. Sprinkle with salt to taste. Add bell peppers to same bag; seal. Turn to mix; set aside. Broil steak 6 to 9 minutes per side for medium rare to medium, turning once. Add bell pepper strips to broiler pan while turning steak.

3. Transfer steak to cutting board; slice across the grain into thin strips. Place steak on warm tortillas. Top with pepper strips and salsa. Serve immediately.

Serving Suggestion: Serve with a tossed green salad and refried beans.

Make-Ahead Time: 1 day before serving
Final Prep and Cook Time: 21 minutes

Carne Asada

TACO TWO-ZIES

Makes 10 tacos

1 pound ground beef
2 packages (1 ounce each) LAWRY'S® Taco Spices & Seasonings
⅔ cup water
1 can (1 pound 14 ounces) refried beans, warmed
10 small flour tortillas (fajita size), warmed to soften
10 jumbo size taco shells, heated according to package directions

TACO TOPPINGS
Shredded lettuce, shredded cheddar cheese and chopped tomatoes

In large skillet, brown ground beef over medium high heat until crumbly; drain fat. Stir in 1 package Taco Spices & Seasonings and water. Bring to a boil; reduce heat to low and cook, uncovered, 10 minutes, stirring occasionally. In medium bowl, mix together beans and remaining package Taco Spices & Seasonings. Spread about ⅓-cup seasoned beans all the way to edges of each flour tortilla. Place a taco shell on center of each bean-tortilla and fold edges up around shell, lightly pressing to 'stick' tortilla to shell. Fill each taco with about 3 tablespoons taco meat. Top with your choice of taco toppings.

Variations: May use lean ground turkey, chicken or pork in place of ground beef. May use LAWRY'S® Chicken Taco Spices & Seasonings or Lawry's® Hot Taco Spices & Seasonings instead of Taco Spices & Seasonings.

Prep. Time: 8 to 10 minutes
Cook Time: 15 minutes

Taco Two-Zies

FAJITA STUFFED SHELLS

Makes 4 servings

¼ cup fresh lime juice
1 clove garlic, minced
½ teaspoon dried oregano leaves
¼ teaspoon ground cumin
½ (6-ounce) boneless beef top round or beef flank steak
1 medium green bell pepper, halved and seeded
1 medium onion, cut in half
12 uncooked jumbo pasta shells (about 6 ounces)
½ cup reduced-fat sour cream
2 tablespoons shredded reduced-fat Cheddar cheese
1 tablespoon minced fresh cilantro
⅔ cup chunky salsa
2 cups shredded leaf lettuce

1. Combine lime juice, garlic, oregano and cumin in shallow nonmetallic dish. Add steak, bell pepper and onion. Cover and refrigerate 8 hours or overnight.

2. Preheat oven to 350°F. Cook pasta shells according to package directions, omitting salt. Drain and rinse well under cold water; set aside.

3. Grill or broil steak and vegetables over medium heat 6 to 8 minutes for medium or until desired doneness, turning once. Cool slightly. Cut steak into thin slices. Chop vegetables. Place steak slices and vegetables in medium bowl. Stir in sour cream, Cheddar cheese and cilantro. Stuff shells evenly with meat mixture, mounding slightly.

4. Arrange shells in 8-inch baking dish. Pour salsa over filled shells. Cover with foil and bake 15 minutes or until heated through. Divide lettuce evenly among 4 plates; arrange 3 shells on each plate.

Fajita Stuffed Shells

CHILI BEEF & RED PEPPER FAJITAS WITH CHIPOTLE SALSA

Makes 2 servings

6 ounces boneless beef top sirloin steak, thinly sliced
½ lime
1½ teaspoons chili powder
½ teaspoon ground cumin
½ cup diced plum tomatoes
¼ cup mild picante sauce
½ canned chipotle chili pepper in adobo sauce
   Nonstick cooking spray
½ cup sliced onion
½ red bell pepper, cut into thin strips
2 (10-inch) fat-free flour tortillas, warmed
¼ cup fat-free sour cream
2 tablespoons chopped fresh cilantro (optional)

1. Place steak on plate. Squeeze lime juice over steak; sprinkle with chili powder and cumin. Coat well; let stand 10 minutes.

2. Meanwhile, to prepare salsa, combine tomatoes and picante sauce in small bowl. Place chipotle on small plate. Using fork, mash completely. Stir mashed chipotle into tomato mixture.

3. Coat 12-inch skillet with cooking spray. Heat over high heat until hot. Add onion and bell pepper; cook and stir 3 minutes or until edges begin to blacken. Remove from skillet. Lightly spray skillet with cooking spray. Add beef; stir-fry 1 minute. Return onion and bell pepper to skillet; cook 1 minute longer.

4. Place ½ the beef mixture in center of each tortilla; fold sides over filling. Top each fajita with ¼ cup salsa, 2 tablespoons sour cream and 1 tablespoon cilantro, if desired.

Note: For a less spicy salsa, use less chipotle chili or eliminate it completely.

Chili Beef & Red Pepper Fajita with Chipotle Salsa

TACO POT PIE

Makes 4 to 6 servings

1 pound ground beef
1 package (1¼ ounces) taco seasoning mix
¼ cup water
1 can (8 ounces) kidney beans, rinsed and drained
1 cup chopped tomato
¾ cup frozen corn, thawed
¾ cup frozen peas, thawed
1½ cups (6 ounces) shredded Cheddar cheese
1 can (11½ ounces) refrigerated corn breadstick dough

1. Preheat oven to 400°F. Brown meat in medium ovenproof skillet over medium-high heat, stirring to separate; drain drippings. Add seasoning mix and water to skillet. Cook over medium-low heat 3 minutes or until most of liquid is absorbed, stirring occasionally.

2. Stir in beans, tomato, corn and peas. Cook 3 minutes or until mixture is hot. Remove from heat; stir in cheese.

3. Unwrap corn breadstick dough; separate into 16 strips. Twist strips, cutting to fit skillet. Arrange attractively over meat mixture. Press ends of dough lightly to edge of skillet to secure. Bake 15 minutes or until corn bread is golden brown and meat mixture is bubbly.

Prep and Cook Time: 30 minutes

TACOS IN PASTA SHELLS

Makes 4 to 6 servings

 1 package (3 ounces) cream cheese with chives
18 jumbo pasta shells
1¼ pounds ground beef
 1 teaspoon salt
 1 teaspoon chili powder
 2 tablespoons butter, melted
 1 cup prepared taco sauce
 1 cup (4 ounces) shredded Cheddar cheese
 1 cup (4 ounces) shredded Monterey Jack cheese
1½ cups crushed tortilla chips
 1 cup sour cream
 3 green onions, chopped
   Leaf lettuce, small pitted ripe olives and cherry tomatoes for garnish

1. Cut cream cheese into ½-inch cubes. Let stand at room temperature until softened. Cook pasta according to package directions. Place in colander and rinse under warm running water. Drain well. Return to saucepan.

2. Preheat oven to 350°F. Butter 13×9-inch baking pan.

3. Cook beef in large skillet over medium-high heat until brown, stirring to separate meat; drain drippings. Reduce heat to medium-low. Add cream cheese, salt and chili powder; simmer 5 minutes.

4. Toss shells with butter. Fill shells with beef mixture. Arrange shells in prepared pan. Pour taco sauce over each shell. Cover with foil.

5. Bake 15 minutes. Uncover; top with Cheddar cheese, Monterey Jack cheese and chips. Bake 15 minutes more or until bubbly. Top with sour cream and onions. Garnish, if desired.

MEXICAN LASAGNA

Makes 8 servings

1 jar (1 pound 10 ounces) RAGÚ® Old World Style® Pasta Sauce
1 pound ground beef
1 can (15¼ ounces) whole kernel corn, drained
4½ teaspoons chili powder
6 (8½-inch) flour tortillas
2 cups shredded Cheddar cheese (about 8 ounces)

1. Preheat oven to 350°F. Set aside 1 cup Ragú Pasta Sauce. In 10-inch skillet, brown ground beef over medium-high heat; drain. Stir in remaining Ragú Pasta Sauce, corn and chili powder.

2. In 13×9-inch baking dish, spread 1 cup sauce mixture. Arrange two tortillas over sauce, overlapping edges slightly. Layer half the sauce mixture and ⅓ of the cheese over tortillas; repeat layers, ending with tortillas. Spread tortillas with reserved sauce.

3. Bake 30 minutes, then top with remaining cheese and bake an additional 10 minutes or until sauce is bubbling and cheese is melted.

Tip: Substitute refried beans for ground beef for a meatless main dish.

Prep Time: 10 minutes
Cook Time: 40 minutes

C. Mexican Lasagna

Shredded Beef Fajitas

Makes 12 servings

1 beef flank steak (about 1½ pounds)
1 cup chopped onion
1 green bell pepper, cut into ½-inch pieces
2 cloves garlic, minced *or* ¼ teaspoon garlic powder
1 package (about 1½ ounces) fajita seasoning mix
1 can (14½ ounces) diced tomatoes with jalapeños, undrained
12 (8-inch) flour tortillas
Toppings: sour cream, guacamole, shredded Cheddar cheese, salsa

Slow Cooker Directions

1. Cut flank steak into 6 portions. Combine beef, onion, bell pepper, garlic and fajita seasoning mix. Add tomatoes with juice. Cover; cook on LOW 8 to 10 hours or on HIGH 4 to 5 hours.

2. Remove beef from slow cooker; shred. Return beef to slow cooker and stir.

3. To serve fajitas, place meat mixture evenly onto flour tortillas. Add toppings as desired; roll up tortillas.

Shredded Beef Fajita

Chicken Dinners

SALSA CHICKEN & RICE SKILLET

Makes 4 servings

1 (6.9-ounce) package RICE-A-RONI® Chicken Flavor
2 tablespoons margarine or butter
1 pound boneless, skinless chicken breasts, cut into 1-inch pieces
1 cup salsa
1 cup frozen or canned corn, drained
1 cup (4 ounces) shredded Cheddar cheese
1 medium tomato, chopped (optional)

1. In large skillet over medium heat, sauté rice-vermicelli mix with margarine until vermicelli is golden brown.

2. Slowly stir in 2 cups water, chicken, salsa and Special Seasonings. Bring to a boil. Reduce heat to low. Cover; simmer 15 minutes.

3. Stir in corn. Cover; simmer 5 minutes or until rice is tender and chicken is no longer pink inside. Top with cheese and tomato, if desired. Cover; let stand 5 minutes for cheese to melt.

Prep Time: 5 minutes
Cook Time: 30 minutes

Salsa Chicken & Rice Skillet

SOUTH-OF-THE-BORDER CUMIN CHICKEN

Makes 4 servings

1 package (16 ounces) frozen bell pepper stir-fry mixture *or* 3 bell peppers, thinly sliced*

4 chicken drumsticks

4 chicken thighs

1 can (14½ ounces) stewed tomatoes, undrained

1 tablespoon mild pepper sauce

2 teaspoons sugar

1¾ teaspoons ground cumin, divided

1¼ teaspoons salt

1 teaspoon dried oregano leaves

¼ cup chopped fresh cilantro leaves

1 to 2 medium limes, cut in wedges

If using fresh bell peppers, add 1 small onion, chopped.

SLOW COOKER DIRECTIONS

1. Place bell pepper mixture in slow cooker; place chicken on top.

2. Combine tomatoes with juice, pepper sauce, sugar, 1 teaspoon cumin, salt and oregano in large bowl. Pour over chicken mixture. Cover; cook on LOW 8 hours or on HIGH 4 hours or until meat is just beginning to fall off bone.

3. Place chicken in shallow serving bowl. Stir remaining ¾ teaspoon cumin into tomato mixture and pour over chicken. Sprinkle with cilantro and serve with lime wedges. Serve over cooked rice or with toasted corn tortillas, if desired.

South-of-the-Border Cumin Chicken

BARBECUED CHICKEN WITH CHILI-ORANGE GLAZE

Makes 4 servings

    1 to 2 dried de arbol chilies*
    ½ cup fresh orange juice
    2 tablespoons tequila
    2 cloves garlic, minced
    1½ teaspoons grated orange peel
    ¼ teaspoon salt
    ¼ cup vegetable oil
    1 broiler-fryer chicken (about 3 pounds), cut into quarters
      Orange slices (optional)
      Cilantro sprigs (optional)

For milder flavor, discard seeds from chili peppers. Since chili peppers can sting and irritate the skin, wear rubber gloves when handling peppers and do not touch eyes. Wash hands after handling chili peppers.

1. Crush chilies into coarse flakes in mortar with pestle. Combine chilies, orange juice, tequila, garlic, orange peel and salt in small bowl. Gradually add oil, whisking continuously, until marinade is thoroughly blended.

2. Arrange chicken in single layer in shallow glass baking dish. Pour marinade over chicken; turn pieces to coat. Marinate, covered, in refrigerator 2 to 3 hours, turning chicken and basting with marinade several times.

3. Prepare charcoal grill for direct cooking or preheat broiler. Drain chicken, reserving marinade. Bring marinade to a boil in small saucepan over high heat; boil 2 minutes. Grill chicken on covered grill or broil, 6 to 8 inches from heat, 15 minutes, brushing frequently with marinade. Turn chicken. Grill or broil 15 minutes more or until chicken is no longer pink in center and juices run clear, brushing frequently with marinade. *Do not baste during last 5 minutes of grilling.* Discard remaining marinade. Garnish with orange slices and cilantro, if desired.

Barbecued Chicken with Chili-Orange Glaze

CHICKEN AND BLACK BEAN SOFT TACOS

Makes 10 tacos

1 package (10) ORTEGA® Soft Taco Dinner Kit (flour tortillas, taco
    seasoning mix and taco sauce)
1 tablespoon vegetable oil
1 pound (3 to 4) boneless, skinless chicken breast halves, cut into
    2-inch strips
1 medium onion, chopped
1 can (15 ounces) black beans, drained
¾ cup whole kernel corn
½ cup water
2 tablespoons lime juice

HEAT oil in large skillet over medium-high heat. Add chicken and onion; cook 4 to 5 minutes or until chicken is no longer pink in center. Stir in taco seasoning mix, beans, corn, water and lime juice. Bring to a boil. Reduce heat to low; cook, stirring occasionally, 5 to 6 minutes or until mixture is thickened.

REMOVE tortillas from outer plastic pouch. Microwave using HIGH (100%) power 10 to 15 seconds or until warm.

FILL each tortilla with ½ cup chicken mixture. Serve with taco sauce.

Chicken and Black Bean Soft Tacos

MILE-HIGH ENCHILADA PIE

Makes 4 to 6 servings

8 (6-inch) corn tortillas
1 jar (12 ounces) prepared salsa
1 can (15½ ounces) kidney beans, rinsed and drained
1 cup shredded cooked chicken
1 cup shredded Monterey Jack cheese with jalapeño peppers

SLOW COOKER DIRECTIONS

Prepare foil handles* for slow cooker; place in slow cooker. Place 1 tortilla on bottom of slow cooker. Top with small amount of salsa, beans, chicken and cheese. Continue layering using remaining ingredients, ending with cheese. Cover; cook on LOW 6 to 8 hours or on HIGH 3 to 4 hours. Pull out by foil handles. Garnish with fresh cilantro and slice of red pepper, if desired.

To make foil handles, tear off three 18×2-inch strips of heavy foil or use regular foil folded to double thickness. Crisscross foil strips in spoke design and place in slow cooker to make lifting of tortilla stack easier.

YA GOTTA EMPANADA

Makes 4 servings (½ empanada each)

1 package (4.4 to 6.8 ounces) Spanish rice mix, prepared according to package directions
1 cup shredded cooked chicken
1 cup (4 ounces) shredded Cheddar cheese
½ cup sliced green onions
¼ cup chopped black olives
1 package (15 ounces) refrigerated pie crust

Combine rice, chicken, cheese, onions and olives in large bowl. Spoon half of rice mixture on half of each pie crust. Fold crust over filling. Seal and crimp edges. Place on baking sheet. Bake at 400°F 20 to 22 minutes or until golden brown. Cut each empanada in half. Serve immediately.

Favorite recipe from **USA Rice**

Mile-High Enchilada Pie

CHICKEN FAJITAS

Makes 4 servings

1 tablespoon vegetable oil
1 large green bell pepper, thinly sliced
1 large red bell pepper, thinly sliced
1 large onion, thinly sliced
1 clove garlic, minced
4 boneless skinless chicken breasts (about 1 pound), cut into ½-inch strips
½ teaspoon dried oregano leaves, crushed
2 tablespoons dry white wine or water
  Salt and black pepper
8 (8-inch) flour tortillas

1. Heat oil in large skillet over medium-high heat. Add green and red peppers, onion and garlic. Cook 3 to 4 minutes or until crisp-tender, stirring occasionally. Remove vegetables with slotted spoon; set aside.

2. Add chicken and oregano to skillet. Cook 4 minutes or until chicken is no longer pink in center, stirring occasionally.

3. Return vegetables to skillet. Add wine. Season with salt and black pepper to taste; cover. Continue cooking 2 minutes or until thoroughly heated.

4. Stack tortillas and wrap in foil. Heat tortillas in 350°F oven 10 minutes or until warm. Fill tortillas with chicken mixture; serve with chunky guacamole, if desired.

Chicken Fajitas

ARROZ CON POLLO

Makes 4 to 6 servings

    4 slices bacon
1½ pounds (about 6) boneless, skinless chicken breasts
    1 cup (1 small) chopped onion
    1 cup (1 small) chopped green bell pepper
    2 large cloves garlic, finely chopped
    2 cups long-grain white rice
    1 jar (16 ounces) ORTEGA® Salsa (any flavor)
1¾ cups (14½-ounce can) chicken broth
    1 cup (8-ounce can) tomato sauce
    1 teaspoon salt
    ½ teaspoon ground cumin
       Chopped fresh parsley

COOK bacon in large saucepan over medium-high heat until crispy; remove from saucepan. Crumble bacon; set aside. Add chicken to saucepan; cook, turning frequently, for 5 to 7 minutes or until golden on both sides. Remove from saucepan; keep warm. Discard all but 2 tablespoons drippings from saucepan.

ADD onion, bell pepper and garlic; cook for 3 to 4 minutes or until crisp-tender. Add rice; cook for 2 to 3 minutes. Stir in salsa, chicken broth, tomato sauce, salt and cumin. Bring to a boil. Place chicken over rice mixture; reduce heat to low. Cover. Cook for 20 to 25 minutes or until most of moisture is absorbed and chicken is no longer pink in center. Sprinkle with bacon and parsley.

Arroz con Pollo

CILANTRO-LIME CHICKEN

Makes 4 servings

1 pound boneless skinless chicken breasts

2 small onions

1 large lime

2 tablespoons canola oil

1 or 2 small green or red jalapeño peppers,* seeded and sliced

1 small piece fresh ginger (1 inch long), peeled and thinly sliced

2 tablespoons chopped fresh cilantro

2 tablespoons reduced-sodium soy sauce

1 to 2 teaspoons sugar

Hot cooked rice

Cilantro sprigs, grated lime peel and red jalapeño pepper* strips for garnish (optional)

*Jalapeño peppers can sting and irritate the skin; wear rubber gloves when handling peppers and do not touch eyes. Wash hands after handling.

1. Rinse chicken and pat dry with paper towels. Cut each chicken breast half into 8 pieces. Cut each onion into 8 wedges.

2. Remove 3 strips of peel from lime with vegetable peeler. Cut lime peel into very fine shreds. Juice lime; measure 2 tablespoons juice. Set aside.

3. Heat wok or large skillet over medium-high heat 1 minute or until hot. Drizzle oil into wok and heat 30 seconds. Add chicken, jalapeño and ginger; stir-fry about 3 minutes or until chicken is no longer pink in center. Reduce heat to medium.

4. Add onions; stir-fry 5 minutes.

5. Add lime peel, juice and chopped cilantro; stir-fry 1 minute. Add soy sauce and sugar to taste; stir-fry until well mixed and heated through. Transfer to serving dish. Serve with rice. Garnish, if desired.

CHICKEN TOSTADAS

Makes 6 servings

6 (8-inch) flour tortillas
  Nonstick cooking spray
1 can (15 ounces) black beans, rinsed and drained
2 teaspoons chili powder, divided
1 teaspoon ground cumin, divided
½ cup hot salsa
12 ounces chicken tenders
2 cups finely chopped tomatoes, drained
1 cup chopped onion
1½ cups (6 ounces) shredded Cheddar cheese
2 cups shredded romaine or iceberg lettuce

1. Preheat oven to 350°F. Place tortillas on two large baking sheets, overlapping as little as possible. Spray both sides of tortillas with cooking spray. Bake 7 minutes. Turn tortillas over and bake 3 minutes more or until no longer soft and flexible.

2. While tortillas are baking, place beans in food processor and process until smooth. Transfer to medium saucepan. Stir in 1 teaspoon chili powder, ½ teaspoon cumin and salsa; bring to a boil over medium heat.

3. Cut chicken into ½-inch pieces. Sprinkle with remaining 1 teaspoon chili powder and remaining ½ teaspoon cumin. Coat large nonstick skillet with cooking spray; heat over medium heat. Add chicken; cook and stir 5 minutes or until cooked through.

4. Spread bean mixture on tortillas to within ½ inch of edges. Top with chicken, tomatoes, onion and cheese. Bake 2 minutes or just until cheese is melted. Top with lettuce; serve immediately.

Note: For a special touch, top each tostada with a dollop of sour cream.

Prep and Cook Time: 28 minutes

CHICKEN PICANTE

Makes 6 servings

½ cup medium-hot chunky taco sauce
¼ cup Dijon mustard
   Juice of 1 medium lime
6 boneless skinless chicken breasts
2 tablespoons butter
   Plain yogurt
   Chopped fresh cilantro and lime slices for garnish (optional)

1. Combine taco sauce, mustard and lime juice in large bowl. Add chicken, turning to coat with marinade. Cover; marinate in refrigerator at least 30 minutes.

2. Melt butter in large skillet over medium heat until foamy.

3. Drain chicken, reserving marinade. Add chicken to skillet in single layer. Cook 10 minutes or until chicken is light brown on both sides. Add reserved marinade to skillet; cook 5 minutes or until chicken is tender and glazed with marinade.

4. Remove chicken to serving platter; keep warm. Boil marinade in skillet over high heat 1 minute; pour over chicken. Serve with yogurt. Garnish, if desired.

Notas

For easier handling, freeze the chicken until it is firm, but not hard. Remove the skin. For each breast half, use a sharp knife to make three or four arched cuts between the meat and the bone, lifting the meat away with your free hand. (Or, slip your fingers between the meat and the bone and work the meat free without the aid of a knife.) When the meat and bone are separated, remove the heavy white tendon that runs along the length of the breast. This will prevent the meat from shrinking as it cooks.

Chicken Picante

CHICKEN ENCHILADA SKILLET CASSEROLE

Makes 4 servings

1 bag (16 ounces) BIRDS EYE® frozen Farm Fresh Mixtures Broccoli, Corn
    & Red Peppers
3 cups shredded cooked chicken
1 can (16 ounces) diced tomatoes, undrained
1 package (1¼ ounces) taco seasoning mix
1 cup shredded Monterey Jack cheese
8 ounces tortilla chips

• In large skillet, combine vegetables, chicken, tomatoes and seasoning mix; bring to boil over medium-high heat.

• Cover; cook 4 minutes or until vegetables are cooked and mixture is heated through.

• Sprinkle with cheese; cover and cook 2 minutes more or until cheese is melted.

• Serve with chips.

Prep Time: 5 minutes
Cook Time: 10 minutes

Chicken Enchilada Skillet Casserole

GRILLED CHILE CHICKEN QUESADILLAS

Makes 12 quesadillas

    2 tablespoons lime juice
    3 cloves garlic, minced
    1 tablespoon ground cumin
    1 tablespoon chili powder
    1 tablespoon vegetable oil
    1 jalapeño pepper, minced
    1 teaspoon salt
    6 skinless boneless chicken thighs
    3 poblano peppers, cut in half, stemmed, seeded
    2 avocados, peeled and sliced
    3 cups (12 ounces) shredded Monterey Jack cheese
   12 (8-inch) flour tortillas
  1½ cups fresh salsa
      Red chiles
      Fresh cilantro sprigs

Combine lime juice, garlic, cumin, chili powder, oil, jalapeño pepper and salt in small bowl; coat chicken with paste. Cover and refrigerate chicken at least 15 minutes. Grill chicken on covered grill over medium-hot KINGSFORD® Briquets 4 minutes per side until no longer pink in center. Grill poblano peppers, skin side down, 8 minutes until skins are charred. Place peppers in large resealable plastic food storage bag; seal. Let stand 5 minutes; remove skin. Cut chicken and peppers into strips. Arrange chicken, peppers, avocado and cheese on half of each tortilla. Drizzle with 2 tablespoons salsa. Fold other half of tortilla over filling. Grill quesadillas on covered grill over medium briquets 30 seconds to 1 minute per side until cheese is melted. Garnish with chiles and cilantro sprigs.

Grilled Chile Chicken Quesadillas

SALSA CHICKEN FAJITAS

Makes 4 servings

2 tablespoons vegetable oil

1 medium onion, sliced

1 medium red bell pepper, cut into ¼-inch strips

1 medium green bell pepper, cut into ¼-inch strips

1 clove garlic, minced

4 boneless skinless chicken breasts (about 1 pound), cut into ¼-inch strips

½ cup chunky salsa

1 tablespoon minced jalapeño pepper*

Salt and black pepper to taste

8 (8-inch) flour tortillas

Guacamole

Shredded mozzarella or Monterey Jack cheese

Additional chunky salsa

Jalapeño peppers can sting and irritate the skin; wear rubber gloves when handling peppers and do not touch eyes. Wash hands after handling.

1. Heat oil in large skillet over medium-high heat. Add onion, bell peppers and garlic. Cook and stir 3 to 4 minutes or until crisp-tender. Remove vegetables with slotted spoon; set aside.

2. Add chicken to skillet. Cook and stir 4 minutes or until chicken is no longer pink in center. Return vegetables to skillet. Add salsa and jalapeño pepper. Season with salt and black pepper; cover. Continue cooking 2 minutes or until thoroughly heated.

3. Stack tortillas and wrap in foil. Heat tortillas in 350°F oven 10 minutes or until warm. Fill tortillas with guacamole, chicken mixture and cheese; top with additional salsa.

Easy Chicken Chalupas

Makes 6 servings

1 roasted chicken (about 2 pounds)
8 flour tortillas
2 cups reduced-fat shredded Cheddar cheese
1 cup mild green chili salsa
1 cup mild red salsa

1. Preheat oven to 350°F. Spray 13×9 ovenproof dish with cooking spray.

2. Remove skin and bones from chicken; discard. Shred chicken meat.

3. Place 2 tortillas in bottom of prepared dish, overlapping slightly. Layer tortillas with 1 cup chicken, ½ cup cheese and ¼ cup of each salsa. Repeat layers, ending with cheese and salsas.

4. Bake casserole 25 minutes or until bubbly and hot.

Notas

Serve this easy main dish with toppings on the side such as sour cream, chopped cilantro, sliced black olives, sliced green onions and sliced avocado.

BLACK BEAN GARNACHAS

Makes 4 servings

1 can (14½ ounces) DEL MONTE® Diced Tomatoes with Garlic & Onion
1 can (15 ounces) black or pinto beans, drained
2 cloves garlic, minced
1 to 2 teaspoons minced jalapeño peppers (optional)
½ teaspoon ground cumin
1 cup cubed grilled chicken
4 flour tortillas
½ cup (2 ounces) shredded sharp Cheddar cheese

1. Combine undrained tomatoes, beans, garlic, jalapeño peppers and cumin in large skillet. Cook over medium-high heat 5 to 7 minutes or until thickened, stirring occasionally. Stir in chicken. Season with salt and pepper, if desired.

2. Arrange tortillas in single layer on grill over medium coals. Spread about ¾ cup chicken mixture over each tortilla. Top with cheese.

3. Cook about 3 minutes or until bottoms of tortillas are browned and cheese is melted. Top with shredded lettuce, diced avocado and sliced jalapeño peppers, if desired.

VARIATION: Prepare chicken mixture as directed above. Place a tortilla in a dry skillet over medium heat. Spread with about ¾ cup chicken mixture; top with 2 tablespoons cheese. Cover and cook about 3 minutes or until bottom of tortilla is browned and cheese is melted. Repeat with remaining tortillas.

Prep Time: 5 minutes
Cook Time: 10 minutes

Black Bean Garnachas

Mexican Lasagna

Makes 6 to 8 servings

4 boneless skinless chicken breasts
2 tablespoons vegetable oil
2 teaspoons chili powder
1 teaspoon ground cumin
1 can (14½ ounces) diced tomatoes with garlic, drained
1 can (8 ounces) tomato sauce
1 teaspoon hot pepper sauce (optional)
1 cup part-skim ricotta cheese
1 can (4 ounces) diced green chilies
¼ cup chopped fresh cilantro, divided
12 (6-inch) corn tortillas
1 cup (4 ounces) shredded Cheddar cheese

Preheat oven to 375°F. Cut chicken into ½-inch pieces.

Heat oil in large skillet over medium heat. Add chicken, chili powder and cumin. Cook 4 minutes or until chicken is tender, stirring occasionally. Stir in diced tomatoes, tomato sauce and hot pepper sauce, if desired; bring to a boil. Reduce heat; simmer 2 minutes.

Combine ricotta cheese, chilies and 2 tablespoons cilantro in small bowl; mix until well blended.

Spoon half of chicken mixture into 12×8-inch baking dish. Top with 6 tortillas, ricotta cheese mixture, remaining 6 tortillas, remaining chicken mixture, Cheddar cheese and remaining 2 tablespoons cilantro. Bake 25 minutes or until heated through.

Mexican Lasagna

SASSY CHICKEN & PEPPERS

Makes 2 servings

2 teaspoons Mexican seasoning*
2 (4-ounce) boneless skinless chicken breasts
2 teaspoons canola oil
1 small red onion, sliced
½ medium red bell pepper, cut into long, thin strips
½ medium yellow or green bell pepper, cut into long, thin strips
¼ cup chunky salsa or chipotle salsa
1 tablespoon lime juice
  Lime wedges (optional)

If Mexican seasoning is not available, substitute 1 teaspoon chili powder, ½ teaspoon ground cumin, ½ teaspoon salt and ⅛ teaspoon ground red pepper.

1. Sprinkle seasoning over both sides of chicken; set aside.

2. Heat oil in large nonstick skillet over medium heat. Add onion; cook 3 minutes, stirring occasionally.

3. Add bell pepper strips; cook 3 minutes, stirring occasionally. Stir salsa and lime juice into vegetables.

4. Push vegetables to edges of skillet; add chicken to skillet. Cook 5 minutes; turn. Continue to cook 4 minutes or until chicken is no longer pink in the center and vegetables are tender.

5. Transfer chicken to serving plates; top with vegetable mixture and garnish with lime wedges, if desired.

Sassy Chicken & Peppers

GREEN CHILI-CHICKEN CASSEROLE

Makes 6 servings

4 cups shredded cooked chicken

1½ cups green enchilada sauce

1 can (10¾ ounces) condensed cream of chicken soup, undiluted

1 container (8 ounces) sour cream

1 can (4 ounces) diced green chilies

½ cup vegetable oil

12 (6-inch) corn tortillas

1½ cups (6 ounces) shredded Colby-Jack cheese, divided

1. Preheat oven to 325°F. Grease 13×9-inch casserole.

2. Combine chicken, enchilada sauce, soup, sour cream and chilies in large skillet. Cook and stir over medium-high heat until warm.

3. Heat oil in separate deep skillet. Fry tortillas just until soft; drain on paper towels. Place 4 tortillas on bottom of prepared casserole. Layer with ⅓ of chicken mixture and ½ cup cheese. Repeat layers twice.

4. Bake 15 to 20 minutes or until cheese is melted and casserole is heated through.

Tip: Shredded Mexican cheese blend can be substituted for Colby-Jack cheese.

Green Chili-Chicken Casserole

SOUTHWEST CHICKEN WITH CILANTRO SALSA

Makes 4 servings

4 boneless skinless chicken breasts
4 tablespoons lime juice, divided
   Black pepper
½ cup lightly packed fresh cilantro, chopped
⅓ cup thinly sliced or minced green onions
¼ to ½ jalapeño pepper,* seeded and minced
2 tablespoons pine nuts, toasted (optional)

*Jalapeño peppers can sting and irritate the skin. Wear rubber gloves when handling peppers and do not touch eyes. Wash hands after handling.

1. Preheat broiler. Spray broiler pan with nonstick cooking spray.

2. Brush chicken with 2 tablespoons lime juice. Place on prepared pan. Sprinkle with black pepper. Broil chicken 2 inches from heat 8 to 10 minutes or until chicken is no longer pink in center.

3. Meanwhile, combine remaining 2 tablespoons lime juice, cilantro, onions, jalapeño pepper and pine nuts, if desired, in small bowl. Serve with chicken.

Notas

*Cilantro is a fresh leafy herb that looks a lot
like Italian parsley. Its distinctive flavor
complements spicy foods, especially Mexican,
Caribbean, Thai and Vietnamese dishes.*

Southwest Chicken with Cilantro Salsa

SPICY SPANISH RICE

Makes 4 servings

1 teaspoon canola oil
1 cup uncooked white rice
1 medium onion, chopped
2 cups chicken stock or canned low-sodium chicken broth, defatted
1 cup GUILTLESS GOURMET® Salsa (Roasted Red Pepper or
  Southwestern Grill)
Green chili pepper strips (optional)

Heat large skillet over medium-high heat until hot. Add oil; swirl to coat skillet.
Add rice; cook and stir until lightly browned. Remove rice to small bowl. Add onion
to same skillet; cook and stir until onion is translucent. Add stock and salsa to
skillet; return rice to skillet. Bring to a boil. Reduce heat to low; cover and simmer
until liquid is absorbed and rice is tender. Serve hot. Garnish with pepper, if
desired.

Spicy Spanish Rice

GREEN RICE PILAF

Makes 4 to 6 servings

2 tablespoons vegetable oil

1 cup uncooked long-grain white rice (not converted)

¼ cup finely chopped white onion

2 fresh poblano or Anaheim chilies,* roasted, peeled, seeded, deveined and chopped

6 thin green onions, thinly sliced

1 clove garlic, minced

¼ teaspoon salt

¼ teaspoon ground cumin

1¾ cups chicken broth

1½ cups shredded queso Chihuahua or Monterey Jack cheese, divided

⅓ cup coarsely chopped fresh cilantro

Cilantro sprig for garnish (optional)

Chilies can sting and irritate the skin; wear rubber gloves when handling peppers and do not touch eyes. Wash hands after handling.

1. Preheat oven to 375°F. Heat oil in large skillet over medium heat until hot. Add rice. Cook and stir 2 minutes or until rice turns opaque.

2. Add white onion; cook and stir 1 minute. Stir in chilies, green onions, garlic, salt and cumin; cook and stir 20 seconds.

3. Stir in broth. Bring to a boil over high heat. Reduce heat to low. Cover and simmer 15 minutes or until rice is almost tender.**

4. Remove skillet from heat. Add 1 cup cheese and chopped cilantro; toss lightly to mix. Transfer to greased 1½-quart baking dish; top with remaining ½ cup cheese.

5. Bake, uncovered, 15 minutes or until rice is tender and cheese topping is melted. Garnish, if desired.

**For plain green rice, complete recipe from this point as follows: Cook rice in skillet 2 to 4 minutes more until tender. Stir in chopped cilantro just before serving; omit cheese.*

Green Rice Pilaf

CONFETTI BLACK BEANS

Makes 6 servings

1 cup dried black beans
3 cups water
1 can (14 ounces) reduced-sodium chicken broth
1 bay leaf
1½ teaspoons olive oil
1 medium onion, chopped
¼ cup chopped red bell pepper
¼ cup chopped yellow bell pepper
2 cloves garlic, minced
1 jalapeño pepper,* finely chopped
1 large tomato, seeded and chopped
½ teaspoon salt
⅛ teaspoon black pepper
Hot pepper sauce (optional)

Jalapeño peppers can sting and irritate the skin; wear rubber gloves when handling peppers and do not touch eyes. Wash hands after handling.

1. Sort and rinse black beans. Cover with water and soak overnight; drain. Place beans in large saucepan with chicken broth; bring to a boil over high heat. Add bay leaf. Reduce heat to low; cover and simmer about 1½ hours or until beans are tender.

2. Heat oil in large skillet over medium heat. Add onion, bell peppers, garlic and jalapeño pepper; cook 8 to 10 minutes or until onion is tender, stirring frequently. Add tomato, salt and black pepper; cook 5 minutes.

3. Add onion mixture to beans; cook 15 to 20 minutes. Remove bay leaf before serving. Serve with hot sauce and garnish, if desired.

Confetti Black Beans

MEXICAN RICE

Makes 8 servings

2 tablespoons butter or margarine
1 cup long-grain white rice*
½ cup chopped onion
2 cloves garlic, finely chopped
1 jar (16 ounces) ORTEGA® Salsa Thick & Chunky
1¼ cups water*
¾ cup (1 large) peeled, shredded carrot
½ cup frozen peas, thawed (optional)

For a quick-cook Mexican Rice, use 4 cups instant rice instead of 1 cup long-grain white rice, and 2½ cups water instead of 1¼ cups water. After salsa mixture comes to a boil, cook for a length of time recommended on instant rice package.

MELT butter in large saucepan over medium heat. Add rice, onion and garlic; cook, stirring occasionally, for 3 to 4 minutes or until rice is golden. Stir in salsa, water, carrot and peas. Bring to a boil. Reduce heat to low; cook, covered, for 25 to 30 minutes or until liquid is absorbed and rice is tender.

Tip: Serve this traditional side dish to complete any Mexican meal.

Mexican Rice

GREEN CHILI RICE

Makes 6 servings

1 cup uncooked white rice
1 can (14½ ounces) fat-free reduced-sodium chicken broth plus water to
    measure 2 cups
1 can (4 ounces) chopped mild green chilies
½ medium yellow onion, peeled and diced
1 teaspoon dried oregano leaves
½ teaspoon salt (optional)
½ teaspoon cumin seeds
3 green onions, thinly sliced
⅓ to ½ cup fresh cilantro leaves

Combine rice, broth, chilies, yellow onion, oregano, salt, if desired, and cumin in
large saucepan. Bring to a boil, uncovered, over high heat. Reduce heat to low;
cover and simmer 18 minutes or until liquid is absorbed and rice is tender. Stir in
green onions and cilantro. Garnish as desired.

Green Chili Rice

Sweets and Drinks

KIWI MARGARITA

Makes 1 serving

3½ ounces MR & MRS T® Margarita Mix
2 ripe kiwi, peeled
1 cup strawberry sorbet
1½ ounces white rum
2 ounces club soda
1 lime, sliced
MR & MRS T® Margarita Salt (optional)

Blend first 5 ingredients in blender on low speed until smooth.* Coat rim of glass with lime and dip in margarita salt, if desired. Pour into glass.

Be careful not to blend too long, as crushed kiwi seeds taste bitter.

Mango Margarita (189) , Kiwi Margarita and Daiquiri (190)

RICE PUDDING MEXICANA

Makes 6 servings

1 package (4-serving size) instant rice pudding
1 tablespoon vanilla
¼ teaspoon ground cinnamon
    Dash ground cloves
¼ cup slivered almonds
    Additional ground cinnamon

1. Prepare rice pudding according to package directions.

2. Remove pudding from heat; stir in vanilla, ¼ teaspoon cinnamon and cloves. Pour evenly into 6 individual dessert dishes.

3. Sprinkle evenly with almonds and additional cinnamon. Serve warm.

Prep and Cook Time: 18 minutes

MEXICAN COFFEE

Makes 8 cups

6 cups hot brewed coffee
1 (14-ounce) can EAGLE BRAND® Sweetened Condensed Milk (NOT evaporated milk)
½ cup coffee liqueur
2 teaspoons vanilla extract
⅓ cup tequila (optional)
    Ground cinnamon (optional)

1. In medium saucepan over medium heat, combine coffee, EAGLE BRAND® and liqueur. Heat through, stirring constantly. Remove from heat; stir in vanilla and tequila, if desired.

2. Sprinkle each serving with cinnamon, if desired. Store covered in refrigerator.

Prep Time: 8 minutes

Rice Pudding Mexicana

FIRE AND ICE

Makes 6 servings

2 cups vanilla ice milk or low-fat ice cream
2 teaspoons finely chopped jalapeño pepper*
1 teaspoon grated lime peel, divided
1 cup water
¼ cup sugar
1 cup peeled and chopped kiwifruit
1 tablespoon lime juice
1 cup fresh raspberries

Jalapeño peppers can sting and irritate the skin; wear rubber gloves when handling peppers and do not touch eyes. Wash hands after handling.

1. Soften ice milk slightly in small bowl. Stir in jalapeño pepper and ½ teaspoon lime peel. Freeze until firm.

2. Combine water, sugar and remaining ½ teaspoon lime peel in small saucepan; bring to a boil. Boil, uncovered, 5 minutes or until reduced by about one third. Remove from heat; cool to room temperature.

3. Place kiwifruit and lime juice in blender or food processor; process until smooth. Stir in water mixture. Pour through fine strainer to remove kiwifruit seeds and lime peel, pressing liquid through strainer with back of spoon. Refrigerate kiwifruit mixture until cold.

4. Pour ¼ cup kiwifruit mixture into each of 6 chilled bowls. Scoop ⅓ cup jalapeño ice milk in center of each bowl. Sprinkle raspberries evenly on top. Garnish with lime peel strips, if desired.

Fire and Ice

CHOCOLATE-RUM PARFAITS

Makes 4 servings

6 to 6½ ounces Mexican chocolate, coarsely chopped*
1½ cups whipping cream, divided
3 tablespoons golden rum (optional)
¾ teaspoon vanilla
    Whipped cream for garnish
    Sliced almonds for garnish
    Cookies (optional)

Or, substitute 6 ounces semisweet chocolate, coarsely chopped, 1 tablespoon ground cinnamon and ¼ teaspoon almond extract.

1. Combine chocolate and 3 tablespoons cream in top of double boiler. Heat over simmering water until chocolate is melted and smooth, stirring occasionally. Gradually stir in rum, if desired; remove top pan from heat. Let stand at room temperature 15 minutes to cool slightly.

2. Combine remaining cream and vanilla in chilled deep bowl. Beat with electric mixer at low speed; gradually increase speed until stiff peaks form.

3. Gently fold whipped cream into cooled chocolate mixture until uniform in color. Spoon chocolate mixture into 4 individual dessert dishes. Refrigerate 2 to 3 hours until firm. Garnish with whipped cream and almonds. Serve with cookies, if desired.

DAIQUIRI

Makes 1 drink

¾ cup MAUNA LA'I® ¡Mango Mango!® Juice Drink
3 tablespoons rum
1 tablespoon ROSE'S® Lime Juice
1 teaspoon sugar
    Ice, as needed

Combine Mauna La'i ¡Mango Mango! Juice Drink, rum, lime juice and sugar in shaker with ice. Pour into tall glass filled with ice.

Chocolate-Rum Parfaits

MEXICAN WEDDING COOKIES

Makes about 4 dozen cookies

1 cup pecan pieces or halves
1 cup (2 sticks) butter, softened
2 cups powdered sugar, divided
2 cups all-purpose flour, divided
2 teaspoons vanilla
⅛ teaspoon salt

1. Place pecans in food processor. Process using on/off pulsing action until pecans are ground but not pasty.

2. Beat butter and ½ cup powdered sugar in large bowl with electric mixer at medium speed until light and fluffy. Gradually add 1 cup flour, vanilla and salt. Beat at low speed until well blended. Stir in remaining 1 cup flour and ground nuts with spoon. Shape dough into ball; wrap in plastic wrap and refrigerate 1 hour or until firm.

3. Preheat oven to 350°F. Shape dough into 1-inch balls. Place 1 inch apart on ungreased cookie sheets.

4. Bake 12 to 15 minutes or until golden brown. Let cookies stand on cookie sheets 2 minutes.

5. Meanwhile, place 1 cup powdered sugar in 13×9-inch glass dish. Transfer hot cookies to powdered sugar. Roll cookies in powdered sugar, coating well. Let cookies cool in sugar.

6. Sift remaining ½ cup powdered sugar over sugar-coated cookies before serving. Store tightly covered at room temperature or freeze up to 1 month.

Mexican Wedding Cookies

LACY TORTILLA HEARTS

Makes 4 servings

4 (8-inch) flour tortillas
3 tablespoons butter or margarine, melted
2 tablespoons vegetable oil
Powdered sugar

1. Cut out ¾- to 1-inch heart shapes evenly throughout tortillas; discard hearts. Place tortillas in 15×10×1-inch jelly-roll pan.

2. Combine butter and oil in small bowl; pour evenly over tortillas. Let stand 15 minutes.

3. Preheat oven to 400°F.

4. Place tortillas in single layer in additional jelly-roll pans or on rimmed baking sheets. Bake 7 to 10 minutes or until crisp. Place tortillas on wire racks or waxed-paper-covered baking sheets. Cool completely. Sprinkle generously with powdered sugar.

Variation: Omit powdered sugar. Combine 1 tablespoon red colored sugar with ⅛ teaspoon cinnamon; mix well. Sprinkle over warm tortillas.

MANGO-LIME COOLER

Makes 4 servings

2 cups cold water
1 cup ice
2 large mangos, peeled, seeded and cubed
½ cup sugar
½ cup freshly squeezed lime juice (about 6 limes)

Combine all ingredients in blender. Blend at high speed until smooth.

Notas

Although largely overlooked by most Americans until recently, mangos are one of the most popular fruits in the world. This lushly aromatic and flavorful fruit is used abundantly in Indian, Mexican and Caribbean cuisines. Native to Southeast Asia, mangos have been cultivated for more than 6,000 years. Now, there are hundreds of varieties, ranging in weight from less than half a pound to four pounds or more. When properly ripe, mangoes have a floral aroma, succulent orange flesh and tropical fruity taste.

CARAMEL FLAN

Makes 6 to 8 servings

1 cup sugar, divided
2 cups half-and-half
1 cup milk
1½ teaspoons vanilla
6 eggs
2 egg yolks
Hot water as needed
Fresh whole and sliced strawberries for garnish (optional)

1. Preheat oven to 325°F. Heat 5½- to 6-cup ring mold in oven 10 minutes or until hot.

2. Heat ½ cup sugar in heavy, medium skillet over medium-high heat 5 to 8 minutes or until sugar is completely melted and deep amber color, stirring frequently. *Do not allow sugar to burn.*

3. Immediately pour caramelized sugar into ring mold. Holding mold with potholder, quickly rotate to coat bottom and sides evenly with sugar. Place mold on wire rack. *Caution: Caramelized sugar is very hot; do not touch it.*

4. Combine half-and-half and milk in heavy 2-quart saucepan. Heat over medium heat until almost simmering; remove from heat. Add remaining ½ cup sugar and vanilla; stir until sugar is dissolved.

5. Lightly beat eggs and egg yolks in large bowl until blended but not foamy; gradually stir in milk mixture. Pour custard into ring mold.

6. Place mold in large baking pan; pour hot water into baking pan to depth of ½ inch. Bake 35 to 40 minutes or until knife inserted into center of custard comes out clean.

7. Remove mold from water bath; place on wire rack. Let stand 30 minutes. Cover and refrigerate 1½ to 2 hours or until thoroughly chilled.

8. To serve, loosen inner and outer edges of flan with tip of small knife. Cover mold with rimmed serving plate; invert and lift off mold. Garnish with strawberries, if desired. Spoon melted caramel over each serving.

Caramel Flan

Toasted Almond Horchata

Makes 8 to 10 servings

3½ cups water, divided
2 (3-inch) cinnamon sticks
1 cup uncooked instant white rice
1 cup slivered almonds, toasted
3 cups cold water
¾ to 1 cup sugar
½ teaspoon vanilla
Lime wedges for garnish (optional)

Combine 3 cups water and cinnamon sticks in medium saucepan. Cover and bring to a boil over high heat. Reduce heat to medium-low. Simmer 15 minutes. Remove from heat; let cool to temperature of hot tap water. Measure cinnamon water to equal 3 cups, adding additional hot water if needed.

Place rice in food processor; process using on/off pulsing action 1 to 2 minutes or until rice is powdery. Add almonds; process until finely ground (mixture will begin to stick together). Remove rice mixture to medium bowl; stir in cinnamon water and cinnamon sticks. Let stand 1 hour or until mixture is thick and rice grains are soft.

Remove cinnamon sticks; discard. Pour mixture into food processor. Add remaining ½ cup water; process 2 to 4 minutes or until mixture is very creamy. Strain mixture through fine-meshed sieve or several layers of dampened cheesecloth into half-gallon pitcher. Stir in 3 cups cold water, sugar and vanilla; stir until sugar is completely dissolved.

To serve, pour over ice cubes, if desired. Garnish with lime wedges, if desired.

Toasted Almond Horchata

PINEAPPLE MARGARITA

Makes 2 servings

⅔ cup DOLE® Pineapple Juice
1½ ounces tequila
1 ounce Triple Sec
  Juice of 1 lemon
  Crushed ice

• Combine pineapple juice, tequila, Triple Sec and lemon juice in blender. Add ice; blend until slushy. Serve in frosted glasses. *(Do not put salt on rim.)*

Notas

Pineapples were first grown in Central and South America. Today most of the domestic supply is grown in Hawaii and Central America. Since they do not ripen after picking, pineapples are picked when ripe and shipped by air to their destination. The distinct pineapple shape has been used as a symbol of hospitality for centuries. This fragrant, juicy, sweet fruit is shaped like a large cylindrical pinecone with long, sharp pointed leaves.

MEXICAN RICE PUDDING

Makes 6 to 8 servings

      7 **cups milk**
      2 **cinnamon sticks**
      3 **tablespoons butter**
  1½ **cups short-grain rice**
      3 **egg yolks**
     ½ **cup sugar**

1. Combine milk and cinnamon sticks in heavy medium saucepan over medium-high heat. Cook until milk begins to simmer; reduce heat to low.

2. Melt butter in large heavy saucepan or Dutch oven. Add rice to butter; stir with wooden spoon and cook 5 minutes or until rice is toasted and turns very pale golden in color. Add 3½ cups of milk and cinnamon sticks to rice; cook over medium heat. Stir occasionally so rice does not burn or stick.

3. When milk is almost completely absorbed, add remaining milk. Stir and cook until liquid is absorbed and rice is tender.

4. Add egg yolks to rice mixture; stir rapidly to incorporate yolks so they do not scramble. Increase temperature to medium-high, stirring constantly to prevent burning. Add sugar; stir until dissolved. Remove from heat. Serve warm, at room temperature or chilled.

Cajeta y Frutas

Makes 12 servings

1 (14-ounce) can sweetened condensed milk
3 cups whipped topping
  Sliced strawberries or peaches, or fresh berries and mint for garnish

1. Pour milk into top of double boiler. Cover with plastic wrap and bring water to a boil over medium-low heat. Simmer 1 to 2 hours, stirring occasionally, until milk is light caramel colored.

2. Pour cooked milk into mixer bowl with paddle attachment. Beat with electric mixer at low speed until milk is smooth and creamy, and at room temperature. Fold in whipped topping and stir just until smooth. Transfer to plastic covered container and refrigerate 2 hours or overnight. Serve is small dish, garnished with fruit and mint.

Cajeta y Frutas

MEXICAN SUGAR COOKIES (POLVORONES)

Makes about 2 dozen cookies

1 cup (2 sticks) butter, softened
½ cup powdered sugar
2 tablespoons milk
1 teaspoon vanilla
1 teaspoon ground cinnamon, divided
1½ to 1¾ cups all-purpose flour
1 teaspoon baking powder
1 cup granulated sugar plus additional as needed
1 square (1 ounce) semisweet chocolate, finely grated

1. Preheat oven to 325°F. Grease cookie sheets; set aside.

2. Beat butter, powdered sugar, milk, vanilla and ½ teaspoon cinnamon in large bowl with electric mixer at medium speed until light and fluffy, scraping down side of bowl once. Gradually add 1½ cups flour and baking powder. Beat at low speed until well blended, scraping down side of bowl once. Stir in additional flour with spoon if dough is too soft to shape.

3. Shape tablespoonfuls of dough into 1¼-inch balls. Place balls 3 inches apart on prepared cookie sheets. Flatten each ball into 2-inch round with bottom of glass dipped in granulated sugar.

4. Bake 20 to 25 minutes or until edges are golden brown. Let stand on cookie sheets 3 to 4 minutes.

5. Meanwhile, combine 1 cup granulated sugar, grated chocolate and remaining ½ teaspoon cinnamon in small bowl. Transfer cookies, one at a time, to sugar mixture; coat both sides. Remove to wire racks; cool completely.

6. Store tightly covered at room temperature or freeze up to 3 months.

Mexican Sugar Cookies (Polvorones)

New Mexican Hot Chocolate

Makes 4 servings

¼ cup unsweetened cocoa powder
¼ cup sugar
½ teaspoon ground cinnamon
¼ teaspoon ground nutmeg
    Dash salt
⅔ cup water
3⅓ cups milk
1 teaspoon vanilla
4 cinnamon sticks or dash ground nutmeg

Combine cocoa, sugar, ground cinnamon, ¼ teaspoon nutmeg, salt and water in 3-quart saucepan. Cook, stirring occasionally, over medium heat until cocoa and sugar are dissolved. Add milk and vanilla. Heat to simmering. Whip mixture with rotary beater or portable electric mixer until frothy. Pour into four mugs. Place one cinnamon stick in each mug or sprinkle each serving lightly with nutmeg.

Biscochitos

Makes 4 to 5 dozen cookies

3 cups all-purpose flour
2 teaspoons anise seeds
1½ teaspoons baking powder
½ teaspoon salt
1 cup (2 sticks) butter
¾ cup sugar, divided
1 egg
¼ cup orange juice
2 teaspoons ground cinnamon

Preheat oven to 350°F. Combine flour, anise seeds, baking powder and salt in medium bowl; set aside. Beat butter in large bowl with electric mixer at medium speed until creamy. Add ½ cup sugar; beat until fluffy. Blend in egg. Gradually add flour mixture alternately with orange juice, mixing well after each addition.

continued on page 208

Top to bottom: New Mexican Hot Chocolate and Biscochitos

Biscochitos, continued

Divide dough in half. Roll out one portion at a time on lightly floured surface to ¼-inch thickness; cover remaining dough to prevent drying. Cut dough with 2- to 2½-inch cookie cutters; gather scraps and re-roll. If dough becomes too soft to handle, refrigerate briefly. Place cookies 1 inch apart on ungreased cookie sheets.

Combine remaining ¼ cup sugar and cinnamon; lightly sprinkle over cookies. Bake 8 to 10 minutes or until edges are lightly browned. Remove to wire racks; cool completely. Store in airtight container.

HONEY SOPAIPILLAS

Makes 16 sopaipillas

¼ **cup plus 2 teaspoons sugar, divided**
½ **teaspoon ground cinnamon**
 2 **cups all-purpose flour**
 2 **teaspoons baking powder**
½ **teaspoon salt**
 2 **tablespoons shortening**
¾ **cup warm water**
  Vegetable oil for deep-frying
  Honey

Combine ¼ cup sugar and cinnamon in small bowl; set aside. Combine flour, remaining 2 teaspoons sugar, baking powder and salt in large bowl. Add shortening. With pastry blender or 2 knives, cut in shortening until mixture resembles fine crumbs. Gradually add water; stir with fork until mixture forms dough. Turn out onto lightly floured board; knead 2 minutes or until smooth. Shape into ball; cover with bowl and let rest 30 minutes.

Divide dough into 4 equal portions; shape each into ball. Flatten each ball to form circle about 8 inches in diameter and ⅛ inch thick. Cut each round into 4 wedges.

Pour oil into electric skillet or deep heavy pan to depth of 1½ inches. Heat to 360°F. Cook dough, 2 pieces at a time, 2 minutes or until puffed and golden brown, turning once during cooking. Remove from oil with slotted spoon; drain on paper towels. Sprinkle with cinnamon-sugar mixture. Repeat with remaining sopaipillas. Serve hot with honey.

BAKED FLAN

Makes 10 (½-cup) servings

    4 cups 2% milk
    6 eggs
    1 cup plus 2 tablespoons EQUAL® SPOONFUL*
 2½ teaspoons vanilla
  ¼ teaspoon salt
    Sliced fresh fruit (optional)
    Fresh mint (optional)

*May substitute 27 packets EQUAL® sweetener.

• Heat milk just to simmering in medium saucepan. Let cool 5 minutes.

• Beat eggs, Equal®, vanilla and salt in large bowl until smooth. Gradually beat in hot milk. Pour mixture into 1½-quart casserole or ten 6-ounce custard cups.

• Place casserole or custard cups in roasting pan. Pour 1 inch of hot water into roasting pan. Bake in preheated 325°F oven 50 to 60 minutes or until knife inserted halfway between center and edge of custard comes out clean.

• Remove casserole or custard cups from roasting pan. Cool to room temperature on wire rack. Refrigerate several hours until well chilled.

• Serve garnished with sliced fresh fruit and mint, if desired.

MEXICAN COFFEE WITH CHOCOLATE AND CINNAMON

Makes 10 to 12 servings

6 cups water
½ cup ground dark roast coffee
2 cinnamon sticks plus more for garnish
2 cups whipping cream, divided
⅓ cup chocolate syrup
¼ cup dark brown sugar, packed
1 teaspoon vanilla
¼ cup powdered sugar
½ teaspoon vanilla
Cinnamon

1. Place water in coffee maker. Add coffee and cinnamon sticks to the filter. Combine 1 cup whipping cream, chocolate syrup, brown sugar and vanilla in coffee pot. Brew coffee mixture so that coffee drips into coffee pot with chocolate cream mixture.

2. Meanwhile, whip remaining 1 cup whipping cream in large bowl. Sprinkle in powdered sugar and vanilla and beat until stiff peaks form. Pour coffee into individual coffee cups and top with whipped cream. Garnish with cinnamon and cinnamon sticks, if desired.

Mexican Coffee with Chocolate and Cinnamon

MEXICAN CHOCOLATE MACAROONS

Makes 3 dozen cookies

1 package (8 ounces) semisweet baking chocolate, divided
1¾ cups plus ⅓ cup whole almonds, divided
¾ cup sugar
1 teaspoon ground cinnamon
1 teaspoon vanilla
2 egg whites

1. Preheat oven to 400°F. Grease cookie sheets; set aside.

2. Place 5 squares chocolate in food processor; process until coarsely chopped. Add 1¾ cups almonds and sugar; process using on/off pulsing action until mixture is finely ground. Add cinnamon, vanilla and egg whites; process just until mixture forms moist dough.

3. Shape dough into 1-inch balls. *(Dough will be sticky.)* Place 2 inches apart on prepared baking sheets. Press 1 whole almond in center of each dough ball.

4. Bake 8 to 10 minutes or just until set. Cool 2 minutes on cookie sheets. Remove to wire racks. Cool completely.

5. Place remaining 3 squares chocolate in small resealable plastic food storage bag; seal. Microwave at HIGH 1 minute; knead bag. Microwave at additional 30-second intervals until chocolate is melted, kneading after each interval. Cut off small corner of bag. Drizzle chocolate over cookies. Let stand until set.

Tip: For longer storage, allow cookies to stand until chocolate drizzle is set. Store in airtight containers.

Prep and Bake Time: 30 minutes

Mexican Chocolate Macaroons

SOUR APPLE MARGARITA

Makes 1 serving

3 ounces MR & MRS T® Margarita Mix
1 ounce sour apple liqueur
1½ ounces tequila
½ ounce ROSE'S® Lime Juice
½ ounce ROSE'S® Triple Sec
½ cup ice
1 lime, sliced
50/50 cinnamon/sugar mixture (optional)

Mix first 6 ingredients in shaker. Shake well. Coat rim of martini glass with lime and dip in cinnamon/sugar mixture, if desired. Strain into glass and serve.

Sour Apple Margarita

Acknowledgments

The publisher would like to thank the companies and organizations listed below for the use of their recipes and photographs in this publication.

ACH FOOD COMPANIES, INC.

Birds Eye® Foods

Bob Evans®

Del Monte Corporation

Dole Food Company, Inc.

Eagle Brand® Sweetened Condensed Milk

Equal® sweetener

The Golden Grain Company®

Guiltless Gourmet®

The Kingsford® Products Co.

Lawry's® Foods

MASTERFOODS USA

Mauna La'i® is a registered trademark of Mott's, LLP

Mr & Mrs T® is a registered trademark of Mott's, LLP

Ortega®, A Division of B&G Foods, Inc.

Reckitt Benckiser Inc.

Rose's® is a registered trademark of Mott's, LLP

Sargento® Foods Inc.

StarKist Seafood Company

Unilever Foods North America

USA Rice Federation

Index

METRIC CONVERSION CHART

VOLUME MEASUREMENTS (dry)

$1/8$ teaspoon = 0.5 mL
$1/4$ teaspoon = 1 mL
$1/2$ teaspoon = 2 mL
$3/4$ teaspoon = 4 mL
1 teaspoon = 5 mL
1 tablespoon = 15 mL
2 tablespoons = 30 mL
$1/4$ cup = 60 mL
$1/3$ cup = 75 mL
$1/2$ cup = 125 mL
$2/3$ cup = 150 mL
$3/4$ cup = 175 mL
1 cup = 250 mL
2 cups = 1 pint = 500 mL
3 cups = 750 mL
4 cups = 1 quart = 1 L

VOLUME MEASUREMENTS (fluid)

1 fluid ounce (2 tablespoons) = 30 mL
4 fluid ounces ($1/2$ cup) = 125 mL
8 fluid ounces (1 cup) = 250 mL
12 fluid ounces ($1 1/2$ cups) = 375 mL
16 fluid ounces (2 cups) = 500 mL

WEIGHTS (mass)

$1/2$ ounce = 15 g
1 ounce = 30 g
3 ounces = 90 g
4 ounces = 120 g
8 ounces = 225 g
10 ounces = 285 g
12 ounces = 360 g
16 ounces = 1 pound = 450 g

DIMENSIONS

$1/16$ inch = 2 mm
$1/8$ inch = 3 mm
$1/4$ inch = 6 mm
$1/2$ inch = 1.5 cm
$3/4$ inch = 2 cm
1 inch = 2.5 cm

OVEN TEMPERATURES

250°F = 120°C
275°F = 140°C
300°F = 150°C
325°F = 160°C
350°F = 180°C
375°F = 190°C
400°F = 200°C
425°F = 220°C
450°F = 230°C

BAKING PAN SIZES

Utensil	Size in Inches/Quarts	Metric Volume	Size in Centimeters
Baking or Cake Pan (square or rectangular)	8×8×2	2 L	20×20×5
	9×9×2	2.5 L	23×23×5
	12×8×2	3 L	30×20×5
	13×9×2	3.5 L	33×23×5
Loaf Pan	8×4×3	1.5 L	20×10×7
	9×5×3	2 L	23×13×7
Round Layer Cake Pan	8×1½	1.2 L	20×4
	9×1½	1.5 L	23×4
Pie Plate	8×1¼	750 mL	20×3
	9×1¼	1 L	23×3
Baking Dish or Casserole	1 quart	1 L	—
	1½ quart	1.5 L	—
	2 quart	2 L	—